JavaScript DOM Manipulation

Interactive Web Development with JavaScript

By
Laurence Lars Svekis

For more content and to learn more, visit
https://basescripts.com/

Summary 7

Introduction 7

JavaScript: DOM Tree and Traversal 8

Introduction to the DOM 8

Understanding the DOM Tree Structure 8

Node Types 9

Parent, Child, and Sibling Relationships 9

DOM Traversal Methods 10

Selecting Nodes 11

Modifying the DOM 11

Multiple Choice Questions with Answers 12

Coding Exercises with Full Solutions 18

JavaScript: Document Object Model (DOM) 23

How the DOM is Structured 23

Accessing the DOM 24

Selecting DOM Elements 24

Modifying DOM Elements 25

Working with Attributes and Styles 26

Event Handling 27

Multiple Choice Questions 27

10 Coding Exercises with Solutions 33

JavaScript: Event Listeners (addEventListener, removeEventListener) 38

Introduction to Event Listeners 39

What are Events? 39

The addEventListener Method 39

The removeEventListener Method 40

Event Object and Its Properties 41

Common Event Types 41

Event Propagation (Bubbling and Capturing) 42

Preventing Default Actions 42

Stopping Event Propagation 43

Multiple Choice Questions 43

10 Coding Exercises with Solutions 50

Conclusion 56

JavaScript: Event Delegation 57

Introduction to Event Delegation 57

How Events Bubble and Capture 57

Why Use Event Delegation 58

Implementing Event Delegation 58

Common Use Cases 59

Benefits of Event Delegation 59

Drawbacks and Considerations 60

Multiple Choice Questions 60

10 Coding Exercises with Full Solutions 67

Conclusion 76

JavaScript: Creating and Manipulating Elements 76

Introduction to DOM Manipulation 77

Creating Elements 77

Appending and Inserting Elements 78

Replacing and Removing Elements 79

Modifying Element Content 80

Working with Attributes 81

Cloning and Document Fragments 81

Performance Considerations 82

Multiple Choice Questions 82

10 Coding Exercises with Full Solutions 90

Conclusion 95

Introduction to Forms and Input Handling in JavaScript 95

Detailed Code Examples 97

Multiple Choice Questions 103

10 Coding Exercises with Full Solutions and Explanations 109

Conclusion 119

JavaScript: Browser Storage (localStorage, sessionStorage, and cookies) 120

Introduction to Browser Storage 120

localStorage 120

sessionStorage 121

Cookies 122

Choosing the Right Storage Mechanism 123

Security Considerations 124

Multiple Choice Questions 124

10 Coding Exercises with Full Solutions and Explanations 130

Conclusion 134

JavaScript: Custom Events (dispatchEvent, CustomEvent, and Event-Driven Programming) 135

Introduction to Event-Driven Programming 135

What are Custom Events? 136

The Event Constructor and CustomEvent 136

Dispatching Custom Events 137

Listening for Custom Events 137

Passing Data with Custom Events 138

Practical Use Cases 138

Multiple Choice Questions 139

10 Coding Exercises with Full Solutions 146

Conclusion 154

JavaScript: Window and Document Objects 154

Introduction to the Window Object 154

Window Methods and Properties 155

Screen Properties 156

The Document Object 157

Document Properties and Methods 157

Multiple Choice Questions 158

10 Coding Exercises with Solutions 165

Conclusion 169

JavaScript: Browser API Integration 169

Geolocation API 170

Web Speech API 171

Web Notifications API 172

Web Workers 172

Multiple Choice Questions 173

10 Coding Exercises with Full Solutions 180

Conclusion 186

About the Author 186

Summary

"JavaScript DOM Manipulation" offers an in-depth guide to understanding and mastering the DOM, a critical aspect of modern web development. From learning the fundamentals of DOM traversal and manipulation to implementing advanced techniques like event delegation and browser API integration, this book equips readers with the skills to create dynamic, interactive web applications. Designed for developers of all levels, this book combines theory with practical application, featuring coding exercises, quizzes, and real-world examples. By the end, readers will have the confidence to apply DOM manipulation techniques in any project, building seamless and engaging user experiences.

Introduction

Welcome to **"JavaScript DOM Manipulation"**, your ultimate guide to mastering one of the most dynamic aspects of modern web development. This book is designed to empower developers of all skill levels by providing a clear and comprehensive understanding of the **Document Object Model (DOM)** — the backbone of dynamic, interactive web pages.

Through hands-on exercises, detailed explanations, and practical examples, you'll learn how to traverse, select, modify, and optimize DOM elements effectively. This book will guide you step-by-step, from the basics of the DOM tree to advanced topics such as event delegation, custom events, and browser API integration.

Whether you're a beginner building your first website or an experienced developer looking to refine your skills, this book offers actionable insights to help you create seamless user experiences. Get ready to unlock the full potential of JavaScript and transform the way you interact with web technologies.

JavaScript: DOM Tree and Traversal

The **Document Object Model (DOM)** represents a web page as a hierarchical tree of nodes. Understanding the DOM and how to traverse it is fundamental for dynamically interacting with the content and structure of a webpage.

Introduction to the DOM

The **Document Object Model (DOM)** is a programming interface for HTML and XML documents. It defines the structure of a document and how scripts can access and manipulate it. When a web page is loaded, the browser creates a DOM that can be modified using JavaScript.

Understanding the DOM Tree Structure

The DOM represents the page as a hierarchical tree:
- **Document** (root of the DOM)
  - **html** element
  - **head** element
  - **title**, **meta**, **link** elements, etc.

8

- **body** element
- **header**, **nav**, **section**, **div**, **p**, **img**, etc.

Each element in the DOM is a node, and these nodes have relationships to each other — parent-child, siblings, ancestors, and descendants.

Node Types

Common node types include:
- **Element nodes**: Represent HTML elements (e.g., `<div>`, `<p>`, `<ul>`).
- **Text nodes**: Represent the text inside elements.
- **Comment nodes**: Represent HTML comments (`<!-- comment -->`).
- **Document node**: The root node representing the entire document.

You can check a node's type using `nodeType`:
- 1 = Element
- 3 = Text node
- 8 = Comment
- 9 = Document

Parent, Child, and Sibling Relationships

- **Parent Node**: The element that directly contains another node.

Example: `<body>` is the parent of `<div>` if `<div>` is inside `<body>`.

- **Child Nodes**: Nodes that are directly contained within another node.

Example: `<li>` elements are children of a `<ul>`.

- **Sibling Nodes**: Nodes that share the same parent.

Example: Two `<li>` elements inside the same `<ul>` are siblings.

DOM Traversal Methods

There are several properties and methods to navigate the DOM tree:

- **Parent Node Access**
  - `node.parentNode`
  - `element.parentElement`
- **Child Node Access**
  - `node.childNodes` (NodeList including text nodes and comments)
  - `element.children` (HTMLCollection of only element nodes)
  - `element.firstChild`, `element.lastChild` (include text nodes)
  - `element.firstElementChild`, `element.lastElementChild` (element nodes only)
- **Sibling Access**
  - `node.previousSibling` / `node.nextSibling` (might include text nodes)
  - `element.previousElementSibling` / `element.nextElementSibling` (elements only)
- **Other Useful Methods**
  - `document.getElementById()`
  - `document.querySelector()`
  - `document.querySelectorAll()`

```
○ element.closest(selector)
○ element.matches(selector)
```
Example:
```
const ul = document.querySelector('ul');
console.log(ul.parentNode); // Logs the
parent of the <ul>, typically the <body>
console.log(ul.children);   // Logs all
element children of the <ul>
```

Selecting Nodes

You can select elements using:
- **ID**: `document.getElementById('myId')`
- **Class**:
`document.getElementsByClassName('myClass')`
- **Tag**: `document.getElementsByTagName('div')`
- **CSS Selectors**:
`document.querySelector('.myClass')`,
`document.querySelectorAll('p')`

Modifying the DOM

Once you've accessed a node, you can modify it:
- **Changing text:** `element.textContent = 'New text'`
- **Changing HTML:** `element.innerHTML = '<strong>Bold text</strong>'`
- **Adding or Removing Elements:**
○ `element.appendChild(node)`

11

- o `element.removeChild(node)`
- o `element.insertBefore(newNode, referenceNode)`

Example:
```
const p = document.createElement('p');
p.textContent = 'This is a new paragraph.';
document.body.appendChild(p);
```

Multiple Choice Questions with Answers

Question 1

What is the DOM?
- A) A database management system
- B) A programming interface for HTML and XML documents
- C) A JavaScript framework
- D) A CSS preprocessor

Answer: B) A programming interface for HTML and XML documents.

Explanation: The DOM allows JavaScript to access and manipulate the structure of a webpage.

Question 2

Which of these returns the first element that matches a CSS selector?
- A) `document.getElementById()`
- B) `document.querySelector()`
- C) `document.querySelectorAll()`
- D) `document.getElementsByTagName()`

Answer: B) `document.querySelector()`

Explanation: `querySelector()` returns the first matching element.

Question 3

Which property would you use to get the parent element of a node?

- A) `node.childNodes`
- B) `node.parentNode`
- C) `node.nextSibling`
- D) `node.firstChild`

Answer: B) `node.parentNode`

Explanation: `parentNode` refers to the node that is the parent of the current node.

Question 4

`document.getElementById('header')` returns what?

- A) A single element
- B) A NodeList
- C) An HTMLCollection
- D) A string

Answer: A) A single element

Explanation: `getElementById()` returns a single element or `null` if not found.

Question 5

Which of the following includes text nodes?

- A) `element.children`
- B) `element.childNodes`
- C) `element.querySelectorAll()`
- D) `element.getElementsByTagName()`

Answer: B) `element.childNodes`
Explanation: `childNodes` includes all child nodes, including text and comment nodes.

Question 6

To get all paragraph elements inside a `<div>`, which method is best?
- A) `div.getElementsByTagName('p')`
- B) `div.getElementById('p')`
- C) `div.querySelector('#p')`
- D) `div.appendChild('p')`

Answer: A) `div.getElementsByTagName('p')`
Explanation: `getElementsByTagName()` returns all matching elements inside the given element.

Question 7

Which property references the node's first element child (ignoring text nodes)?
- A) `element.firstChild`
- B) `element.firstElementChild`
- C) `element.previousElementSibling`
- D) `element.lastElementChild`

Answer: B) `element.firstElementChild`
Explanation: `firstElementChild` returns the first child that is an element, not a text node.

Question 8

How do you remove a child node?
- A) `element.removeChild(child)`
- B) `element.deleteChild(child)`
- C) `element.destroyChild(child)`

- D) `element.parentNode(child)`

Answer: A) `element.removeChild(child)`

Explanation: `removeChild()` is used to remove a specified child node.

Question 9

Which node type number represents an Element node?
- A) 1
- B) 3
- C) 8
- D) 9

Answer: A) 1

Explanation: `nodeType` of 1 represents an Element node.

Question 10

What does `document.documentElement` represent?
- A) The head element
- B) The root `<html>` element
- C) The body element
- D) The title element

Answer: B) The root `<html>` element

Explanation: `document.documentElement` returns the `<html>` element.

Question 11

`element.nextElementSibling` returns:
- A) The next node (including text) in the same parent
- B) The next element node in the same parent
- C) The next child node of the element
- D) The parent node of the element

Answer: B) The next element node in the same parent

Question 12

```
document.createElement('div'):
```
- A) Selects an existing `<div>` element
- B) Creates a new `<div>` element in memory
- C) Inserts a new `<div>` directly into the DOM
- D) Returns a list of `<div>` elements

Answer: B) Creates a new `<div>` element in memory

Question 13

Which of the following returns an HTMLCollection?
- A) `document.querySelectorAll('.class')`
- B)
`document.getElementsByClassName('class')`
- C) `document.querySelector('.class')`
- D) `document.createElement('div')`

Answer: B)
`document.getElementsByClassName('class')`

Question 14

`nodeType` of 3 represents:
- A) Element node
- B) Text node
- C) Comment node
- D) Document node

Answer: B) Text node

Question 15

How do you replace an existing node with a new node?

- A) `parentElement.replaceNode(newNode, oldNode)`
- B) `parentElement.replaceChild(newNode, oldNode)`
- C) `parentElement.changeNode(oldNode, newNode)`
- D) `parentElement.setChild(newNode, oldNode)`

Answer: B) `parentElement.replaceChild(newNode, oldNode)`

Question 16

To move from a child node to its parent, use:
- A) `node.parentNode`
- B) `node.childNodes`
- C) `node.nextSibling`
- D) `node.ownerDocument`

Answer: A) `node.parentNode`

Question 17

Which method returns a `NodeList` instead of an `HTMLCollection`?
- A) `document.getElementsByTagName()`
- B) `document.getElementsByClassName()`
- C) `document.querySelectorAll()`
- D) `document.getElementById()`

Answer: C) `document.querySelectorAll()`

Question 18

Which property returns all child **elements** of an element node (no text nodes)?

- A) `element.childNodes`
- B) `element.children`
- C) `element.querySelectorAll('*')`
- D) `element.textContent`

Answer: B) `element.children`

Question 19

`element.innerHTML = 'Hello!'`:

- A) Gets the HTML content
- B) Sets the HTML content
- C) Removes the element
- D) Appends a new child

Answer: B) Sets the HTML content

Question 20

`document.body` returns:

- A) The `<body>` element
- B) The `<head>` element
- C) The `<html>` element
- D) The `<div>` element

Answer: A) The `<body>` element

Coding Exercises with Full Solutions

Exercise 1: Accessing Parent Node

Task: Select a `<li>` element and log its parent's tag name.
HTML:
```
<ul id="list">
```

```
<li>Item 1</li>
<li id="secondItem">Item 2</li>
<li>Item 3</li>
</ul>
```
Solution:
```
const secondItem =
document.getElementById('secondItem');
console.log(secondItem.parentNode.tagName);
// Output: UL
```
Explanation:
parentNode returns the `<ul>` element that contains `<li id="secondItem">`.

Exercise 2: Accessing Children

Task: Get all direct children of a `<ul>` and log their text content.
Solution:
```
const ul = document.getElementById('list');
const children = ul.children; //
HTMLCollection
for (let i = 0; i < children.length; i++) {
  console.log(children[i].textContent);
}
```
Explanation:
ul.children returns only element nodes. Iterating through them logs their text.

Exercise 3: Accessing Siblings

Task: Select the second `<li>` and log the text of its next sibling element.
Solution:

```
const secondItem =
document.getElementById('secondItem');
const nextSibling =
secondItem.nextElementSibling;
console.log(nextSibling.textContent);
// Output: Item 3
```
Explanation:
nextElementSibling gives the next <li> in the list.

Exercise 4: Creating and Appending Elements

Task: Create a new <li> element and append it to the
<ul>.
Solution:
```
const newLi = document.createElement('li');
newLi.textContent = 'Item 4';
ul.appendChild(newLi);
```
Explanation:
document.createElement('li') creates a new <li>
which we then append to the existing <ul>.

Exercise 5: Removing an Element

Task: Remove the second <li> from the <ul>.
Solution:
```
ul.removeChild(secondItem);
```
Explanation:
removeChild() removes the specified child node from
the parent node.

Exercise 6: Replacing a Node

Task: Replace the first <li> with a new <li> element
containing "New Item 1".

Solution:
```
const firstLi = ul.children[0];
const replacementLi =
document.createElement('li');
replacementLi.textContent = 'New Item 1';
ul.replaceChild(replacementLi, firstLi);
```
Explanation:
`replaceChild()` replaces the existing first `<li>` with
`replacementLi`.

Exercise 7: Selecting Elements by CSS Selector

Task: Use `querySelector()` to select the first `<li>` in
the `<ul>` and log its text.
Solution:
```
const firstListItem =
document.querySelector('#list li');
console.log(firstListItem.textContent);
```
Explanation:
`querySelector('#list li')` selects the first `<li>`
inside `#list`.

Exercise 8: Counting Child Nodes

Task: Log how many child nodes (including text nodes)
the `<ul>` has.
Solution:
```
console.log(ul.childNodes.length);
```
Explanation:
`childNodes` includes text and comment nodes, so the
count might be different than `children.length`.

Exercise 9: Navigating Up and Down the DOM Tree

Task: From the third `<li>`, access its parent `<ul>` and then find the first `<li>`.
Solution:
```
const thirdLi = ul.children[2]; // Assuming
Item 3 is at index 2
const parentUl = thirdLi.parentNode;
const firstLiAgain =
parentUl.firstElementChild;
console.log(firstLiAgain.textContent);
// Output: New Item 1 (if replaced
previously)
```
Explanation:
We move up to the `<ul>` from the third `<li>` and then get the first child `<li>` of that `<ul>`.

Exercise 10: Modifying Inner HTML

Task: Change the inner HTML of the `<ul>` to have three `<li>` items: "A", "B", "C".
Solution:
```
ul.innerHTML = `
   <li>A</li>
   <li>B</li>
   <li>C</li>
 `;
```
Explanation:
`innerHTML` replaces the entire content of `<ul>` with the specified HTML string.
This comprehensive guide and exercises cover everything you need to know about the DOM tree, traversal, and manipulation in JavaScript. You can now confidently navigate and modify the DOM for dynamic, interactive web pages.

JavaScript: Document Object Model (DOM)

The **Document Object Model (DOM)** is a crucial part of web development. It provides an interface for JavaScript to interact with the structure and content of a web page. With the DOM, you can select elements, change their styles, attributes, and content, and respond to user interactions. The **Document Object Model** is a platform- and language-neutral interface that allows programs (like JavaScript) to dynamically access and update the content, structure, and style of documents. When the browser loads a webpage, it creates a DOM representation, where each part of the document (e.g., `<p>` elements, `<div>` elements, text, etc.) is a node in a tree.

How the DOM is Structured

The DOM represents the HTML document as a tree of nodes:

- **Document Node**: The root node (e.g., `document` in JavaScript).
- **Element Nodes**: Represent HTML elements (e.g., `<body>`, `<div>`, `<p>`).
- **Text Nodes**: Represent the text content within elements.
- **Attribute Nodes**: Represent attributes on elements (e.g., `id`, `class`).

The hierarchy looks like this:

```
Document
  └── html
```

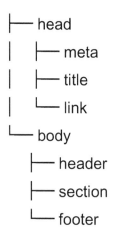

```
├── head
│   ├── meta
│   ├── title
│   └── link
└── body
    ├── header
    ├── section
    └── footer
```

Accessing the DOM

JavaScript can access the DOM through the `document` object. For example:

```
console.log(document); // Logs the Document object
```

Selecting DOM Elements

You can select DOM elements using several methods:
1. **By ID**:
   ○ `document.getElementById('myId')`
   Returns the single element with the given `id`.

```
const element =
document.getElementById('heading');
console.log(element.textContent);
```

2. **By Class Name**:

○ `document.getElementsByClassName('myClass')`

Returns an HTMLCollection of elements.

```
const elements =
document.getElementsByClassName('item');
console.log(elements[0].textContent);
```

3. **By Tag Name**:

○ `document.getElementsByTagName('p')`

Returns an HTMLCollection of <p> elements.

```
const paragraphs =
document.getElementsByTagName('p');
console.log(paragraphs.length);
```

4. **Using Query Selectors**:

○ `document.querySelector('selector')` returns the first matching element.

○ `document.querySelectorAll('selector')` returns a NodeList of all matching elements.

```
const firstParagraph =
document.querySelector('p');
const allItems =
document.querySelectorAll('.item');
console.log(allItems.length);
```

Common Selectors:

- `#id` for ID
- `.class` for class
- `tagname` for elements
- Complex selectors like `div > p`, `ul li.item`, etc.

Modifying DOM Elements

Once an element is selected, you can modify it:

Changing Text Content:
```
const heading =
document.getElementById('heading');
heading.textContent = 'New Heading';
```
Changing HTML Content:
```
heading.innerHTML = '<span>Updated
Heading</span>';
```
Creating and Appending Elements:
```
const newParagraph =
document.createElement('p');
newParagraph.textContent = 'A new
paragraph';
document.body.appendChild(newParagraph);
```
Removing Elements:
```
document.body.removeChild(newParagraph);
```
Replacing Elements:
```
const oldElement =
document.getElementById('old');
const newElement =
document.createElement('div');
newElement.textContent = 'I replaced the
old element';
oldElement.parentNode.replaceChild(newEleme
nt, oldElement);
```

Working with Attributes and Styles

Attributes:
```
const link = document.querySelector('a');
link.setAttribute('href',
'https://www.example.com');
console.log(link.getAttribute('href'));
```

Classes:
```
link.classList.add('highlight');
link.classList.remove('highlight');
```
Styles:
```
heading.style.color = 'red';
heading.style.fontSize = '24px';
```

Event Handling

You can attach event listeners to elements to respond to user actions.
```
const button =
document.getElementById('myButton');
button.addEventListener('click', function()
{
  console.log('Button clicked!');
});
```

Multiple Choice Questions

Question 1

Which method returns the first element in the document that matches the specified selector?
- A) `document.getElementById()`
- B) `document.querySelector()`
- C) `document.querySelectorAll()`
- D) `document.getElementsByClassName()`

Answer: B) `document.querySelector()`

Explanation: `querySelector()` returns the first matching element.

Question 2

`document.getElementById('test')` returns what?
- A) A NodeList
- B) An HTMLCollection
- C) A single DOM element or null
- D) An array of elements

Answer: C) A single DOM element or null

Explanation: `getElementById()` always returns a single element or `null` if not found.

Question 3

How to select all elements with the class "item"?
- A) `document.getElementById('item')`
- B) `document.querySelectorAll('.item')`
- C) `document.getElementsByTagName('item')`
- D) `document.getElementsByClassName('#item')`

Answer: B) `document.querySelectorAll('.item')`

Explanation: `.item` is the correct selector for elements with class `item`.

Question 4

`document.querySelectorAll('p')` returns:
- A) The first `<p>` element
- B) A NodeList of all `<p>` elements
- C) An HTMLCollection of `<p>` elements
- D) A string of HTML

Answer: B) A NodeList of all `<p>` elements

Question 5

Which property would you use to change the text inside an element?
- A) `element.value`
- B) `element.textContent`
- C) `element.innerHtml`
- D) `element.setText()`

Answer: B) `element.textContent`
Explanation: `textContent` sets the text of the element, `innerHTML` sets HTML content.

Question 6

Which method adds a new child node to the DOM?
- A) `appendChild()`
- B) `insertBefore()`
- C) `removeChild()`
- D) `replaceChild()`

Answer: A) `appendChild()`

Question 7

What does `document.createElement('div')` do?
- A) Selects an existing `<div>` element
- B) Creates a new `<div>` element but does not add it to the DOM
- C) Inserts a `<div>` directly into the body
- D) Returns an HTMLCollection of `<div>` elements

Answer: B) Creates a new `<div>` element but does not add it to the DOM

Question 8

Which method returns an HTMLCollection of elements?
- A) `document.querySelectorAll('.class')`
- B) `document.getElementsByClassName('class')`
- C) `document.querySelector('.class')`
- D) `element.closest('.class')`

Answer: B) `document.getElementsByClassName('class')`
Explanation: `getElementsByClassName()` returns an HTMLCollection.

Question 9

To remove a child node, you use:
- A) `removeChild()`
- B) `deleteChild()`
- C) `unappendChild()`
- D) `popChild()`

Answer: A) `removeChild()`

Question 10

`element.innerHTML = '<p>Hi</p>'`:
- A) Gets the inner HTML
- B) Sets the inner HTML
- C) Removes the element
- D) Appends a new child element

Answer: B) Sets the inner HTML

Question 11

Which attribute method sets a new attribute or modifies an existing one?
- A) `element.getAttribute()`

- B) `element.hasAttribute()`
- C) `element.setAttribute()`
- D) `element.updateAttribute()`

Answer: C) `element.setAttribute()`

Question 12

How to add an event listener to a button click?
- A) `button.onClick() = function(){}`
- B) `button.addEventListener('click', function(){})`
- C) `button.listenClick(function(){})`
- D) `button.onclickEvent(function(){})`

Answer: B) `button.addEventListener('click', function(){})`

Question 13

Which method returns the parent node of a given node?
- A) `node.childNodes`
- B) `node.parentNode`
- C) `node.previousSibling`
- D) `node.nextSibling`

Answer: B) `node.parentNode`

Question 14

What does `document.body` return?
- A) The `<html>` element
- B) The `<head>` element
- C) The `<title>` element
- D) The `<body>` element

Answer: D) The `<body>` element

Question 15

What does `element.classList.add('active')` do?
- A) Replaces all classes with 'active'
- B) Adds the 'active' class to the element's class list if not already present
- C) Removes the 'active' class
- D) Toggles the 'active' class

Answer: B) Adds the 'active' class to the element's class list if not already present

Question 16

`querySelector()` uses what kind of syntax to find elements?
- A) XPath
- B) JSON Path
- C) CSS Selector Syntax
- D) Regex

Answer: C) CSS Selector Syntax

Question 17

What is returned by `document.querySelectorAll('.item')` if no elements match?
- A) null
- B) undefined
- C) An empty NodeList
- D) An empty HTMLCollection

Answer: C) An empty NodeList

Question 18

Which is the correct way to set inline styles?
- A) `element.style = "color: red;"`
- B) `element.setAttribute('style', 'color:red;')`
- C) `element.style.color = 'red';`
- D) `element.changeStyle('color', 'red')`

Answer: C) `element.style.color = 'red';`

Question 19

What method can insert a node before a reference node?
- A) `element.appendChild()`
- B) `element.insertBefore(newNode, referenceNode)`
- C) `element.replaceChild()`
- D) `element.moveChild()`

Answer: B) `element.insertBefore(newNode, referenceNode)`

Question 20

What does `element.textContent` do?
- A) Sets HTML content
- B) Sets text content, stripping any HTML
- C) Returns all child elements
- D) Returns only attribute names

Answer: B) Sets text content, stripping any HTML

10 Coding Exercises with Solutions

Exercise 1: Selecting an Element by ID

Task: Given an HTML element with `id="title"`, select it and log its text content.
HTML:
```
<h1 id="title">Hello World</h1>
```
Solution:
```
const title =
document.getElementById('title');
console.log(title.textContent); // "Hello World"
```
Explanation:
`getElementById()` returns the element with the specified ID.

Exercise 2: Selecting Multiple Elements by Class

Task: Log the number of elements with class `item`.
HTML:
```
<ul>
  <li class="item">Item 1</li>
  <li class="item">Item 2</li>
  <li class="item">Item 3</li>
</ul>
```
Solution:
```
const items =
document.getElementsByClassName('item');
console.log(items.length); // 3
```
Explanation:
`getElementsByClassName()` returns an HTMLCollection of all elements with the given class.

Exercise 3: Using querySelector

Task: Select the first `<p>` element on the page and change its text to "Updated!".

HTML:
```
<p>Original Text</p>
<p>Another paragraph</p>
```
Solution:
```
const p = document.querySelector('p');
p.textContent = 'Updated!';
```
Explanation:
querySelector('p') selects the first <p> element found.

Exercise 4: Using querySelectorAll

Task: Select all elements with class .item and log their text content.
HTML:
```
<div class="item">Box 1</div>
<div class="item">Box 2</div>
<div class="item">Box 3</div>
```
Solution:
```
const allItems =
document.querySelectorAll('.item');
allItems.forEach(item =>
console.log(item.textContent));
```
Explanation:
querySelectorAll() returns a NodeList. We can use forEach() to iterate over it.

Exercise 5: Creating and Appending Elements

Task: Create a new <li> element with text "New Item" and append it to a <ul>.
HTML:
```
<ul id="myList">
```

```
  <li>Existing Item</li>
</ul>
```
Solution:
```
const ul =
document.getElementById('myList');
const newLi = document.createElement('li');
newLi.textContent = 'New Item';
ul.appendChild(newLi);
```
Explanation:
`createElement()` creates a new element.
`appendChild()` adds it to the end of the parent.

Exercise 6: Removing an Element

Task: Remove the first `<li>` from the `<ul>`.
Solution:
```
const firstLi = ul.querySelector('li');
ul.removeChild(firstLi);
```
Explanation:
`removeChild()` removes a specified child from the parent node.

Exercise 7: Replacing a Child Element

Task: Replace the first `<li>` with a new `<li>` that says "Replaced Item".
HTML:
```
<ul id="myList">
  <li>Old Item</li>
  <li>Another Item</li>
</ul>
```
Solution:
```
const oldLi = ul.querySelector('li');
```

```
const newLi2 =
document.createElement('li');
newLi2.textContent = 'Replaced Item';
ul.replaceChild(newLi2, oldLi);
```
Explanation:
`replaceChild()` replaces one child node with another.

Exercise 8: Changing Attributes

Task: Change the `href` attribute of a link to
`"https://www.google.com"`.
HTML:
```
<a id="myLink"
href="https://www.example.com">Click Me</a>
```
Solution:
```
const link =
document.getElementById('myLink');
link.setAttribute('href',
'https://www.google.com');
```
Explanation:
`setAttribute()` updates the specified attribute.

Exercise 9: Working with ClassList

Task: Add the class `highlight` to all `<p>` elements on the
page.
HTML:
```
<p>Paragraph 1</p>
<p>Paragraph 2</p>
```
Solution:
```
const paragraphs =
document.querySelectorAll('p');
```

```
paragraphs.forEach(p =>
p.classList.add('highlight'));
```
Explanation:
`classList.add('highlight')` adds the class to each paragraph.

Exercise 10: Inline Styles

Task: Change the color of all `.item` elements to red.
HTML:
```
<div class="item">Box 1</div>
<div class="item">Box 2</div>
```
Solution:
```
const boxes =
document.querySelectorAll('.item');
boxes.forEach(box => {
  box.style.color = 'red';
});
```
Explanation:
`style` can be used to set inline CSS properties directly on elements.

JavaScript: Event Listeners (addEventListener, removeEventListener)

Event listeners are a fundamental part of JavaScript programming, enabling you to respond to user interactions and other events in the browser. By mastering event listeners, you can create highly interactive and dynamic web applications.

Introduction to Event Listeners

An **event listener** is a function that runs in response to a specific event happening on a DOM element. Events can be user actions (clicks, key presses) or browser triggers (page load, resize).

What are Events?

Events are signals that something has happened. Examples:

- **User events**: click, keyup, mousemove
- **Browser events**: load, resize, scroll
- **Form events**: submit, change, focus, blur

The addEventListener Method

addEventListener(type, listener, [options]) attaches an event handler to a specific event type on a target element.

Syntax:

```
element.addEventListener('click',
function(event) {
  console.log('Element clicked!');
});
```

Parameters:

- **type**: A string representing the event type (e.g., 'click').
- **listener**: The callback function that will be executed when the event occurs.

- **options**: Optional. An object or boolean that specifies event properties like `capture`, `once`, and `passive`.

Example:

```
const btn =
document.getElementById('myButton');
btn.addEventListener('click', () => {
  console.log('Button was clicked!');
});
```

Using Options:

```
btn.addEventListener('click', handler, {
once: true });
// The event listener is removed
automatically after the first click.
```

The removeEventListener Method

`removeEventListener(type, listener, [options])` removes a previously added event listener. It's crucial that the parameters match exactly what was used in `addEventListener`.

Syntax:

```
element.removeEventListener('click',
handler);
```

Important Note: To remove a listener, the function (listener) must be referenced by the same variable or function name. Anonymous functions cannot be easily removed because you have no reference to them.

Example:

```
function clickHandler() {
  console.log('Button clicked!');
}
```

```
btn.addEventListener('click',
clickHandler);
// Later in code
btn.removeEventListener('click',
clickHandler);
```

Event Object and Its Properties

When an event occurs, the browser passes an **event object** to the event handler. This object contains information about the event, such as:

• event.target: The element that triggered the event.
• event.currentTarget: The element that the listener is attached to.
• event.type: The type of the event (e.g., 'click').
• event.preventDefault(): Prevents the default browser action.
• event.stopPropagation(): Stops the event from bubbling up the DOM.

Example:
```
btn.addEventListener('click', (event) => {
  console.log('Clicked element:',
event.target);
});
```

Common Event Types

• **Mouse events**: click, dblclick, mousedown, mouseup, mouseenter, mouseleave, mousemove

- **Keyboard events**: keydown, keyup, keypress
- **Form events**: submit, change, focus, blur, input
- **Window events**: load, resize, scroll, unload

Event Propagation (Bubbling and Capturing)

- **Bubbling**: Events start at the target element and bubble up through its ancestors.
- **Capturing**: Events start from the top of the document and go down to the target element.

By default, most events bubble. You can control this with the capture option in addEventListener.

Example:

```
document.body.addEventListener('click',
function() {
  console.log('Body clicked!');
}, true); // Using capture phase
```

Preventing Default Actions

Some events have default browser actions, like clicking a link navigating the page. You can prevent these default actions using event.preventDefault().

Example:

```
const link =
document.getElementById('myLink');
link.addEventListener('click', (event) => {
  event.preventDefault();
  console.log('Link default action
prevented.');
```

```
});
```

Stopping Event Propagation

You can use `event.stopPropagation()` to stop the
event from bubbling up the DOM.
Example:
```
childElement.addEventListener('click',
(event) => {
  event.stopPropagation();
  console.log('Event will not bubble up!');
});
```

Multiple Choice Questions

Question 1

Which method is used to attach an event listener to a DOM
element?
- A) `element.attachEvent()`
- B) `element.onEvent()`
- C) `element.addEventListener()`
- D) `element.eventListener()`

Answer: C) `element.addEventListener()`
Explanation: The modern standard method is
`addEventListener()`.

Question 2

Which method removes a previously added event listener?

- A) `element.removeEventListener()`
- B) `element.detachEvent()`
- C) `element.unbindEvent()`
- D) `element.deleteEvent()`

Answer: A) `element.removeEventListener()`

Explanation: `removeEventListener()` removes an event listener added with `addEventListener()`.

Question 3

Which parameter in `addEventListener()` determines the event type?
- A) The first parameter
- B) The second parameter
- C) The third parameter
- D) No parameters needed

Answer: A) The first parameter

Explanation: The first parameter is the event type string (e.g., `'click'`).

Question 4

Which property of the event object returns the element that triggered the event?
- A) `event.trigger`
- B) `event.source`
- C) `event.target`
- D) `event.currentTarget`

Answer: C) `event.target`

Explanation: `event.target` is the actual element that triggered the event.

Question 5

What does `once: true` option do in `addEventListener()`?
- A) It prevents the event from firing at all.
- B) It removes the event listener after it fires once.
- C) It stops event propagation.
- D) It changes the event type to one-time event.

Answer: B) It removes the event listener after it fires once.

Explanation: The `once` option removes the listener after the first invocation.

Question 6

Can you remove an event listener if it was defined as an anonymous function directly in `addEventListener()`?
- A) Yes, easily with `removeEventListener()`.
- B) Yes, but only if the event is never fired.
- C) No, you need a named function reference.
- D) No, `removeEventListener()` doesn't exist.

Answer: C) No, you need a named function reference.

Explanation: Without a named reference, you cannot remove it since you must pass the same function.

Question 7

Which method would you use to prevent a form from submitting?
- A) `event.stopPropagation()`
- B) `event.preventDefault()`
- C) `event.stopImmediatePropagation()`
- D) `event.cancelBubble()`

Answer: B) `event.preventDefault()`

Explanation: `preventDefault()` stops the browser's default action, such as submitting a form.

Question 8

Event bubbling means:
- A) The event travels from the top (document) down to the target.
- B) The event travels from the target element up through its ancestors.
- C) The event stays only at the target element.
- D) The event fires multiple times.

Answer: B) The event travels from the target element up through its ancestors.

Explanation: Bubbling phase moves upward through the DOM.

Question 9

To listen for the event in the capturing phase, you set which option to true?
- A) `{capture: true}`
- B) `{once: true}`
- C) `{passive: true}`
- D) `{bubbles: true}`

Answer: A) `{capture: true}`

Explanation: The `capture` option determines whether the listener is in the capturing phase.

Question 10

What does `event.stopPropagation()` do?
- A) Stops the browser's default action.
- B) Stops the event from reaching any other listeners.
- C) Restarts the event chain.
- D) Converts the event from bubbling to capturing phase.

Answer: B) Stops the event from reaching any other listeners.

Explanation: `stopPropagation()` prevents further event propagation.

Question 11

Which property of the event object tells you the type of event?
- A) `event.type`
- B) `event.kind`
- C) `event.eventType`
- D) `event.category`

Answer: A) `event.type`

Explanation: `type` returns a string with the event type (e.g., `'click'`).

Question 12

When attaching multiple event listeners to the same element for the same event type:
- A) Only the first one will fire.
- B) All of them will fire in the order they were added.
- C) The last one will override the others.
- D) This causes an error.

Answer: B) All of them will fire in the order they were added.

Explanation: Multiple listeners for the same event all fire in sequence.

Question 13

`event.currentTarget` refers to:
- A) The element that initiated the event.

- B) The element on which the event listener is currently invoked.
- C) The window object.
- D) The top-most element that handled the event.

Answer: B) The element on which the event listener is currently invoked.

Explanation: `currentTarget` is always the element that the event listener was attached to.

Question 14

To remove an event listener, what must match the original `addEventListener()` call?
- A) The event type and the element ID.
- B) The event type, the listener function, and the same options.
- C) Only the event type.
- D) Only the listener function.

Answer: B) The event type, the listener function, and the same options.

Explanation: All parameters must match to remove the listener successfully.

Question 15

If `capture` is set to `true`, when is the event listener executed?
- A) During the bubbling phase.
- B) During the capturing phase.
- C) After all bubbling listeners.
- D) Never.

Answer: B) During the capturing phase.

Explanation: `capture: true` runs the listener during the capturing phase.

Question 16

The `click` event is a:
- A) Keyboard event
- B) Mouse event
- C) Form event
- D) Window event

Answer: B) Mouse event

Explanation: `click` is triggered by mouse interactions (or similar pointer events).

Question 17

If you do not call `preventDefault()` on a link click event, the browser will:
- A) Do nothing
- B) Reload the page
- C) Navigate to the link's href
- D) Throw an error

Answer: C) Navigate to the link's href

Explanation: By default, clicking a link navigates to its `href` destination.

Question 18

To attach an event listener that removes itself after being triggered once, you can use:
- A) {once: true}
- B) {capture: true}
- C) {passive: true}
- D) No such option exists

Answer: A) {once: true}

Explanation: The once option automatically removes the listener after one execution.

Question 19

Which event is fired when a user presses a key down?
- A) keydown
- B) keyup
- C) keypress
- D) input

Answer: A) keydown

Explanation: keydown occurs when a key is initially pressed down.

Question 20

passive: true indicates what?
- A) The event listener won't call preventDefault().
- B) The event listener will run only once.
- C) The event listener runs in capture phase.
- D) The event listener is removed after firing.

Answer: A) The event listener won't call preventDefault().

Explanation: passive: true hints that the event listener will not invoke preventDefault().

10 Coding Exercises with Solutions

Exercise 1: Click Event Listener

Task: Add a click event listener to a button with id="myButton" that logs "Button clicked!" to the console.

HTML:
```
<button id="myButton">Click Me</button>
```
Solution:
```
const btn =
document.getElementById('myButton');
btn.addEventListener('click', () => {
  console.log('Button clicked!');
});
```
Explanation:
When the button is clicked, the anonymous function runs, logging the message.

Exercise 2: Removing an Event Listener

Task: Add a `click` event listener that logs "Hello" and then remove it after clicking twice.
HTML:
```
<button id="myButton">Click Twice</button>
```
Solution:
```
const btn =
document.getElementById('myButton');
let count = 0;
function sayHello() {
  count++;
  console.log('Hello');
  if (count === 2) {
    btn.removeEventListener('click',
sayHello);
  }
}
btn.addEventListener('click', sayHello);
```

Explanation:
After the second click, `removeEventListener()` is called to stop future logs.

Exercise 3: Using Event Object

Task: On a paragraph click, log the tag name of the clicked element using `event.target`.
HTML:
```
<p id="myParagraph">Click me</p>
```
Solution:
```
const p =
document.getElementById('myParagraph');
p.addEventListener('click', (event) => {
  console.log('Clicked element:',
event.target.tagName);
});
```
Explanation:
`event.target.tagName` prints the element name in uppercase (e.g., P).

Exercise 4: Prevent Default

Task: Prevent a link from navigating away when clicked.
HTML:
```
<a id="myLink"
href="https://www.example.com">Go to
example.com</a>
```
Solution:
```
const link =
document.getElementById('myLink');
link.addEventListener('click', (event) => {
  event.preventDefault();
  console.log('Navigation prevented.');
```

```
});
```

Explanation:
`preventDefault()` stops the link's default navigation behavior.

Exercise 5: Event Bubbling

Task: Add `click` listeners to a `<div>` and a `<button>` inside it. Log messages to show the order of bubbling.
HTML:
```
<div id="container">
  <button id="innerButton">Click
Inside</button>
</div>
```
Solution:
```
const container =
document.getElementById('container');
const innerButton =
document.getElementById('innerButton');
container.addEventListener('click', () => {
  console.log('Container clicked');
});
innerButton.addEventListener('click', () =>
{
  console.log('Button clicked');
});
```
Explanation:
Clicking the button logs "Button clicked" then "Container clicked" due to event bubbling.

Exercise 6: Stopping Propagation

Task: Stop the event from bubbling up when the button is clicked.
Solution:
```
innerButton.addEventListener('click',
(event) => {
  event.stopPropagation();
  console.log('Button clicked, propagation
stopped');
});
```
Explanation:
Now "Container clicked" won't log because propagation is stopped at the button.

Exercise 7: Once Option

Task: Add a `click` listener to a button that only fires once.
HTML:
```
<button id="onceButton">Click Me
Once</button>
```
Solution:
```
const onceBtn =
document.getElementById('onceButton');
onceBtn.addEventListener('click', () => {
  console.log('This will only log once!');
}, { once: true });
```
Explanation:
The listener is automatically removed after the first click.

Exercise 8: Named Handler for Removal

Task: Attach a named click handler and then remove it after 3 clicks.
HTML:

```
<button id="counterButton">Click me 3
times</button>
```
Solution:
```
const counterBtn =
document.getElementById('counterButton');
let clickCount = 0;
function clickHandler() {
  clickCount++;
  console.log(`Clicked ${clickCount}
times`);
  if (clickCount === 3) {
    counterBtn.removeEventListener('click',
clickHandler);
  }
}
counterBtn.addEventListener('click',
clickHandler);
```
Explanation:
After the third click, the handler is removed.

Exercise 9: Keyboard Event

Task: Listen for the keydown event on document and log
the pressed key.
Solution:
```
document.addEventListener('keydown',
(event) => {
  console.log(`Key pressed: ${event.key}`);
});
```
Explanation:
Every key press logs the corresponding key.

Exercise 10: Form Submit Prevention

Task: Prevent a form from submitting and log a message instead.

HTML:

```
<form id="myForm" action="/submit"
method="POST">
  <input type="text" name="username">
  <button type="submit">Submit</button>
</form>
```

Solution:

```
const form =
document.getElementById('myForm');
form.addEventListener('submit', (event) =>
{
  event.preventDefault();
  console.log('Form submission
prevented!');
});
```

Explanation:

`preventDefault()` stops the form submission, allowing custom handling.

Conclusion

By understanding how to use `addEventListener` and `removeEventListener`, handling event objects, preventing default actions, and controlling event propagation, you can create interactive web pages that respond to user actions seamlessly. The provided multiple-choice questions and coding exercises reinforce these concepts and help you master event-driven programming in JavaScript.

JavaScript: Event Delegation

Event delegation is a powerful technique that allows you to handle events more efficiently by taking advantage of event propagation (bubbling and capturing phases). Instead of attaching event listeners to multiple child elements, you attach a single event listener to a parent element and let the event "bubble up" or "capture down" to handle it at a higher level. This can greatly improve performance and maintainability in large applications.

Introduction to Event Delegation

Event delegation leverages the way events propagate through the DOM. Rather than adding listeners to many individual child elements, you place a single listener on a common ancestor. When an event occurs on a child, it bubbles up to the ancestor, where your single event listener handles it. You check the `event.target` (or use `event.currentTarget` and logic) to determine which child triggered the event, then act accordingly.

Example Concept: Instead of adding a `click` event listener to each button in a list, you add one `click` listener to the parent `<ul>` and determine which `<li>` or `<button>` was clicked by inspecting the event object.

How Events Bubble and Capture

- **Capturing Phase:** The event travels from the document root down to the target element.

- **Bubbling Phase:** The event then bubbles up from the target back up through its ancestors.

By default, most event listeners are registered in the bubbling phase. Event delegation typically relies on this bubbling behavior.

Why Use Event Delegation

- **Performance:** Attaching one listener to a parent instead of multiple listeners to many children reduces memory usage and improves performance, especially in dynamic lists.
- **Maintainability:** Makes code simpler. When items are added or removed dynamically, no need to add or remove listeners every time.
- **Flexibility:** Handle events for all current and future children with a single listener.

Implementing Event Delegation

Step-by-Step:
1. Identify a common parent element of the child elements that need event handling.
2. Attach a single event listener to the parent.
3. In the event handler, use `event.target` or `event.currentTarget` to detect which child element triggered the event.
4. Based on the element clicked, run appropriate logic.
Example:
```
<ul id="menu">
  <li data-action="edit">Edit</li>
  <li data-action="delete">Delete</li>
```

```
    <li data-action="share">Share</li>
</ul>
<script>
const menu =
document.getElementById('menu');
menu.addEventListener('click', (event) => {
  if (event.target.tagName === 'LI') {
    const action =
event.target.dataset.action;
    console.log(`You chose to ${action}`);
  }
});
</script>
```

If you click on a <li>, the event handler on the #menu ul element runs, identifies which <li> was clicked, and then performs the corresponding action.

Common Use Cases

• Handling clicks on a list of items (e.g., navigation menus, galleries, todo lists).
• Dynamically generated content (tables, form inputs).
• UI components like dropdowns, modals, and carousels where content changes frequently.
• Handling events on a grid or multiple similar elements without attaching separate listeners.

Benefits of Event Delegation

• **Scalability:** One listener replaces many.

- **Dynamic Content:** No need to reassign event listeners to newly created child elements.
- **Easier Cleanup:** Fewer listeners means less complicated code when removing or altering elements.

Drawbacks and Considerations

- **Event.target vs Event.currentTarget:** Make sure to differentiate these properties. `event.target` is where the event originated, while `event.currentTarget` is the element the listener is bound to.
- **Hit Testing Complexities:** If you rely on `event.target`, ensure that the target is the expected node type (e.g., you might click on a nested `<span>` inside a `<li>`).
- **Performance Overkill for Small Projects:** For very small static pages, event delegation might be unnecessary complexity.

Multiple Choice Questions

Question 1

What is event delegation?
- A) A method to attach event listeners directly to child elements.
- B) A technique of adding a single event listener to a common ancestor to handle events from its children.
- C) A way to prevent default browser actions.
- D) A method to stop event propagation.

Answer: B) A technique of adding a single event listener to a common ancestor.

Explanation: Event delegation uses the concept of event bubbling to handle events from multiple child elements with one parent listener.

Question 2

Which property helps identify the element that actually triggered the event?
- A) `event.currentTarget`
- B) `event.target`
- C) `event.type`
- D) `event.stopPropagation`

Answer: B) `event.target`

Explanation: `event.target` references the actual element that initiated the event.

Question 3

Event delegation commonly relies on which event phase?
- A) Capturing
- B) Bubbling
- C) Target
- D) None of the above

Answer: B) Bubbling

Explanation: By default, events bubble up, allowing the parent to handle events fired by its children.

Question 4

What is a primary advantage of event delegation?
- A) It increases memory usage.
- B) It complicates event handling.
- C) It reduces the number of event listeners needed.

- D) It prevents any event from firing.

Answer: C) It reduces the number of event listeners needed.

Explanation: One listener at a parent can handle multiple child elements, improving performance.

Question 5

Which method would you use to stop the event from bubbling further?
- A) `event.preventDefault()`
- B) `event.stopPropagation()`
- C) `event.stopImmediatePropagation()`
- D) `event.cancelBubble()`

Answer: B) `event.stopPropagation()`

Explanation: `stopPropagation()` stops the event from moving further up the DOM.

Question 6

In event delegation, where is the event listener typically placed?
- A) On every child element.
- B) On a common ancestor (often a parent element).
- C) On the document object only.
- D) On the window object.

Answer: B) On a common ancestor (often a parent element).

Question 7

If an `<li>` inside a `<ul>` is clicked, by default the event will:
- A) Only trigger on the `<li>`.
- B) Trigger on the `<li>` and then bubble up to the `<ul>`.

- C) Trigger on the `<ul>` but not the `<li>`.
- D) Not trigger at all unless specified.

Answer: B) Trigger on the `<li>` and then bubble up to the `<ul>`.

Question 8

`event.currentTarget` refers to:
- A) The element that triggered the event.
- B) The element on which the event listener is registered.
- C) Always the `document`.
- D) Always the `window`.

Answer: B) The element on which the event listener is registered.

Question 9

For event delegation, checking `event.target` is important because:
- A) It tells you which listener was added.
- B) It identifies which child element was interacted with.
- C) It always equals `event.currentTarget`.
- D) It stops events from firing.

Answer: B) It identifies which child element was interacted with.

Question 10

Which event phases exist in the DOM?
- A) Capturing, Target, Bubbling
- B) Loading, Rendering, Unloading
- C) Start, Middle, End
- D) Parent, Child, Sibling

Answer: A) Capturing, Target, Bubbling

Question 11

Event delegation can help when adding new elements dynamically because:
- A) You must add new listeners every time.
- B) The single parent listener also handles newly added children.
- C) It prevents new elements from ever receiving events.
- D) It stops the default behavior of new elements.

Answer: B) The single parent listener also handles newly added children.

Question 12

`event.preventDefault()` does what?
- A) Stops the event from bubbling.
- B) Prevents the default browser action (like following a link).
- C) Stops all event listeners on the page.
- D) Removes the event target from the DOM.

Answer: B) Prevents the default browser action.

Question 13

Event delegation is best used with:
- A) Many static elements that never change.
- B) A small number of elements with no dynamic behavior.
- C) Large dynamic lists, menus, or tables where items are frequently added or removed.
- D) Situations where events never bubble.

Answer: C) Large dynamic lists or menus.

Question 14

If you rely on `event.target`, you should ensure:
- A) The target is always the parent element.
- B) The target is what you expect (e.g., check `tagName` or `className`).
- C) That you never call `stopPropagation()`.
- D) That the element has an inline listener.

Answer: B) Ensure the target is what you expect.

Question 15

To use event delegation with `click` events on list items, you attach a `click` listener to:
- A) Every `li`.
- B) The `ul` or `ol` that contains the `li` elements.
- C) The `document`.
- D) The `li` that appears first.

Answer: B) The `ul` or `ol` containing the `li`.

Question 16

Event delegation reduces performance overhead by:
- A) Removing all events from the document.
- B) Only using capturing phase.
- C) Reducing the number of event listeners attached to the DOM.
- D) Using `once: true` option.

Answer: C) Reducing the number of event listeners.

Question 17

To identify a clicked element in event delegation, you might use:
- A) `event.target.classList`
- B) `event.target.dataset`
- C) `event.target.id`
- D) All of the above.

Answer: D) All of the above.

Explanation: Any of these properties could help identify the clicked element.

Question 18

If the structure of the DOM changes (e.g., items added/removed), with event delegation you need to:
- A) Reassign all listeners.
- B) Do nothing, the single parent listener still works.
- C) Remove and reattach the parent listener.
- D) Use `stopPropagation()` to reset the listeners.

Answer: B) Do nothing, the single parent listener still works.

Question 19

Which event property can you check to ensure you are handling the right kind of element?
- A) `event.type`
- B) `event.target.tagName`
- C) `event.currentTarget`
- D) `event.defaultPrevented`

Answer: B) `event.target.tagName`

Question 20

Which is NOT an advantage of event delegation?
- A) Less memory usage.

- B) Handles dynamic elements easily.
- C) Only works with `click` events.
- D) Cleaner code structure.

Answer: C) Only works with `click` events.
Explanation: Event delegation can be used with many event types, not just clicks.

10 Coding Exercises with Full Solutions

Exercise 1: Basic Event Delegation

Task: Given a `<ul>` with multiple `<li>` items, attach a single click event to the `ul` and log the text of the clicked `<li>`.

HTML:
```html
<ul id="myList">
  <li>Apple</li>
  <li>Banana</li>
  <li>Cherry</li>
</ul>
```
Solution:
```javascript
const myList =
document.getElementById('myList');
myList.addEventListener('click', (event) =>
{
  if (event.target.tagName === 'LI') {
    console.log('You clicked:',
event.target.textContent);
  }
});
```

Explanation:
We check `event.target.tagName` to ensure we only react if an `<li>` was clicked.

Exercise 2: Dynamic Content

Task: Start with an empty `<ul>` and a button. Each time the button is clicked, add a new `<li>`. Use event delegation on the `<ul>` to handle clicks on `<li>`s.

HTML:

```
<ul id="dynamicList"></ul>
<button id="addItem">Add Item</button>
```

Solution:

```
const dynamicList =
document.getElementById('dynamicList');
const addItemButton =
document.getElementById('addItem');
let count = 0;
addItemButton.addEventListener('click', ()
=> {
  count++;
  const newLi =
document.createElement('li');
  newLi.textContent = `Item ${count}`;
  dynamicList.appendChild(newLi);
});
dynamicList.addEventListener('click',
(event) => {
  if (event.target.tagName === 'LI') {
    console.log(`Clicked on:
${event.target.textContent}`);
  }
});
```

Explanation:

The single listener on dynamicList handles clicks on any
`<li>` added later.

Exercise 3: Using Data Attributes

Task: Clicks on `<li>` elements should log the action
specified in their `data-action` attribute using delegation.
HTML:

```
<ul id="actionList">
  <li data-action="edit">Edit</li>
  <li data-action="delete">Delete</li>
  <li data-action="share">Share</li>
</ul>
```

Solution:

```
const actionList =
document.getElementById('actionList');
actionList.addEventListener('click',
(event) => {
  const li = event.target.closest('li');
  if (li) {
    console.log(`Action:
${li.dataset.action}`);
  }
});
```

Explanation:

`event.target.closest('li')` ensures we get the
`<li>` even if a child element (like a `<span>`) was clicked.

Exercise 4: Handling Multiple Event Types

Task: Use event delegation to handle both `click` and `dblclick` events on a list of items.

HTML:

```
<ul id="multiEventList">
  <li>First</li>
  <li>Second</li>
  <li>Third</li>
</ul>
```

Solution:

```
const multiEventList =
document.getElementById('multiEventList');
multiEventList.addEventListener('click',
(event) => {
  if (event.target.tagName === 'LI') {
    console.log('Clicked:',
event.target.textContent);
  }
});
multiEventList.addEventListener('dblclick',
(event) => {
  if (event.target.tagName === 'LI') {
    console.log('Double Clicked:',
event.target.textContent);
  }
});
```

Explanation:
Two listeners on the parent handle two different events via delegation.

Exercise 5: Stopping Propagation

Task: Inside the `<ul>`, there's a nested `<span>`. Clicking the span should still select the `<li>`. Prevent the event from reaching an outer container `<div>`.

HTML:

```html
<div id="container">
  <ul id="nestList">
    <li>Item <span>(click here)</span></li>
    <li>Another Item <span>(click
here)</span></li>
  </ul>
</div>
```

Solution:

```javascript
const nestList =
document.getElementById('nestList');
const container =
document.getElementById('container');
container.addEventListener('click', () => {
  console.log('Container clicked');
});
nestList.addEventListener('click', (event)
=> {
  const li = event.target.closest('li');
  if (li) {
    event.stopPropagation();
    console.log('LI clicked:',
li.textContent);
  }
});
```

Explanation:

`stopPropagation()` prevents the event from bubbling to `container`.

Exercise 6: Filtering Targets

Task: Add a single `click` listener to a parent `<div>` containing buttons. Only log the text of the `<button>` elements, ignore other clicks inside the `<div>`.
HTML:
```
<div id="btnContainer">
  <button>Button 1</button>
  <span>Not a button</span>
  <button>Button 2</button>
</div>
```
Solution:
```
const btnContainer =
document.getElementById('btnContainer');
btnContainer.addEventListener('click',
(event) => {
  if (event.target.tagName === 'BUTTON') {
    console.log('Button clicked:',
event.target.textContent);
  }
});
```
Explanation:
Check `tagName` to ensure the target is a button.

Exercise 7: Delegation with Class Check

Task: Only respond if the clicked element has a class `clickable`.
HTML:
```
<div id="classContainer">
  <div class="clickable">Clickable
Div</div>
  <div>Non-clickable Div</div>
</div>
```

Solution:
```
const classContainer =
document.getElementById('classContainer');
classContainer.addEventListener('click',
(event) => {
  if
(event.target.classList.contains('clickable
')) {
    console.log('Clicked a clickable
element');
  }
});
```
Explanation:
Use `classList.contains()` to verify the class.

Exercise 8: Using Closest for Delegation

Task: An `<ul>` with `<li>` elements contains nested tags.
Use `closest('li')` to ensure we always find the correct
`<li>` when clicked.
HTML:
```
<ul id="closestList">
  <li><a href="#">Link in item 1</a></li>
  <li><span>Text in item 2</span></li>
</ul>
```
Solution:
```
const closestList =
document.getElementById('closestList');
closestList.addEventListener('click',
(event) => {
  const li = event.target.closest('li');
  if (li) {
```

73

```
      console.log('You clicked on:',
li.textContent);
   }
});
```

Explanation:

`closest('li')` finds the nearest ancestor `<li>`, handling clicks on nested elements.

Exercise 9: Delegation with Removed Elements

Task: Items can be removed by clicking them. Use delegation so that even newly added items can be removed without adding extra listeners.

HTML:
```
<ul id="removalList">
  <li>Item 1</li>
  <li>Item 2</li>
</ul>
<button id="addNew">Add New Item</button>
```
Solution:
```
const removalList =
document.getElementById('removalList');
const addNew =
document.getElementById('addNew');
let itemCount = 2;
addNew.addEventListener('click', () => {
  itemCount++;
  const newLi =
document.createElement('li');
  newLi.textContent = `Item ${itemCount}`;
  removalList.appendChild(newLi);
});
```

```
removalList.addEventListener('click',
(event) => {
  const li = event.target.closest('li');
  if (li) {
    li.remove();
    console.log(`${li.textContent}
removed`);
  }
});
```
Explanation:
One listener handles removal. Newly added items are also
handled without extra code.

Exercise 10: Delegation with Different Actions

Task: In a list, some `<li>` elements have `data-action="remove"`, others have `data-action="highlight"`. Use one listener to perform the respective actions on click.

HTML:
```
<ul id="actionableList">
  <li data-action="remove">Remove me</li>
  <li data-action="highlight">Highlight
me</li>
  <li data-action="remove">Remove me</li>
</ul>
```
Solution:
```
const actionableList =
document.getElementById('actionableList');
actionableList.addEventListener('click',
(event) => {
  const li = event.target.closest('li');
```

```
  if (li) {
    const action = li.dataset.action;
    if (action === 'remove') {
      li.remove();
      console.log('Item removed');
    } else if (action === 'highlight') {
      li.style.backgroundColor = 'yellow';
      console.log('Item highlighted');
    }
  }
});
```
Explanation:
A single listener decides what to do based on `data-action`.

Conclusion

Event delegation simplifies event handling by leveraging event bubbling. It reduces the need for multiple listeners, improves performance, and makes it easier to handle dynamic content. By mastering event delegation, you can create more efficient and maintainable JavaScript applications.

JavaScript: Creating and Manipulating Elements

Creating and manipulating elements in JavaScript is essential for building dynamic, interactive web pages. By using the DOM (Document Object Model) API, you can programmatically create, insert, remove, and modify

HTML elements. This guide covers the fundamental methods and properties for DOM manipulation, along with examples, multiple-choice questions, and practical exercises.

Introduction to DOM Manipulation

The DOM represents a webpage as a tree of nodes. JavaScript can access this tree through the `document` object and manipulate elements to:
- Dynamically create new elements
- Insert them into the page
- Modify existing elements' content, styles, and attributes
- Remove elements from the DOM

Creating Elements

Use `document.createElement(tagName)` to create a new element node:

```
const newDiv =
document.createElement('div');
```

This creates a `<div>` element in memory, not yet in the DOM. To place it into the webpage, you must append it to an existing node.

You can also create text nodes using `document.createTextNode('some text')`:

```
const textNode =
document.createTextNode('Hello World');
```

Appending and Inserting Elements

appendChild()

`parent.appendChild(child)` adds a node to the end of the parent's list of children.

```
const container =
document.getElementById('container');
const paragraph =
document.createElement('p');
paragraph.textContent = 'This is a new
paragraph.';
container.appendChild(paragraph);
```

insertBefore()

`parent.insertBefore(newNode, referenceNode)` inserts `newNode` before `referenceNode`.

```
const reference =
document.getElementById('referenceElement')
;
const newItem =
document.createElement('li');
newItem.textContent = 'New Item';
reference.parentNode.insertBefore(newItem,
reference);
```

append() and prepend()

- `element.append(...nodes)` appends one or more nodes or strings at the end.
- `element.prepend(...nodes)` inserts them at the beginning.

```
const list =
document.getElementById('myList');
list.prepend(document.createTextNode('Start
: '));
list.append(document.createTextNode('
:End'));
```

Replacing and Removing Elements

replaceChild()

parent.replaceChild(newNode, oldNode) replaces
the oldNode with newNode.
```
const oldElement =
document.getElementById('old');
const newElement =
document.createElement('div');
newElement.textContent = 'Replaced
content';
oldElement.parentNode.replaceChild(newEleme
nt, oldElement);
```

removeChild()

parent.removeChild(child) removes child from
the parent's list of children.
```
const item =
document.getElementById('itemToRemove');
item.parentNode.removeChild(item);
```

remove()

`element.remove()` removes the element from the DOM.

```
const item =
document.getElementById('itemToRemove');
item.remove();
```

Modifying Element Content

innerHTML

`element.innerHTML` gets or sets the HTML markup inside an element. Setting `innerHTML` replaces all the element's content.

```
const div =
document.getElementById('content');
div.innerHTML = '<strong>Hello</strong>';
```

Caution: Setting `innerHTML` can lead to security issues if you insert unsanitized content. Also, it can re-parse and replace all child elements, which is less efficient for minor updates.

textContent

`element.textContent` gets or sets the text inside an element without parsing HTML.

```
div.textContent = 'Plain text only';
```

innerText

`element.innerText` considers CSS styling and returns the visible text. It's less commonly used due to performance considerations and differences from `textContent`.

Working with Attributes

Use `element.setAttribute(name, value)` and `element.getAttribute(name)` to manipulate attributes.

```
const link = document.createElement('a');
link.setAttribute('href',
'https://www.example.com');
link.textContent = 'Visit Example';
document.body.appendChild(link);
```

You can also use property access for standard attributes:

```
link.href = 'https://www.example.com';
```

Cloning and Document Fragments

cloneNode()

`element.cloneNode(deep)` returns a copy of the node. If `deep` is `true`, it copies all descendants.

```
const original =
document.getElementById('original');
const clone = original.cloneNode(true);
document.body.appendChild(clone);
```

DocumentFragment

`document.createDocumentFragment()` creates a lightweight container for holding multiple nodes before appending them to the DOM. This reduces reflows and improves performance when inserting large numbers of elements.

```
const fragment =
document.createDocumentFragment();
for (let i = 0; i < 100; i++) {
  const li = document.createElement('li');
  li.textContent = 'Item ' + i;
  fragment.appendChild(li);
}
document.getElementById('list').appendChild
(fragment);
```

Performance Considerations

- **Batch Updates:** Use DocumentFragment or perform all changes before appending to the live DOM.
- **Avoid Unnecessary Reflows:** Minimizing DOM insertions and removals can improve performance.
- **Use textContent Over innerHTML When Possible:** If you don't need HTML parsing, textContent is faster and safer.

Multiple Choice Questions

Question 1

Which method creates a new element in the DOM?
- A) document.createElement()
- B) document.makeElement()
- C) document.buildElement()
- D) document.newElement()

Answer: A) `document.createElement()`

Explanation: `createElement()` is the standard method to create a new DOM element.

Question 2

Which method inserts a new node at the end of a parent element?

- A) `parent.appendChild(node)`
- B) `parent.insertChild(node)`
- C) `parent.pushChild(node)`
- D) `parent.appendNode(node)`

Answer: A) `parent.appendChild(node)`

Explanation: `appendChild()` adds a node to the end of the parent's child list.

Question 3

Which property sets or gets the HTML content of an element?

- A) `element.textContent`
- B) `element.innerHTML`
- C) `element.value`
- D) `element.outerHTML`

Answer: B) `element.innerHTML`

Explanation: `innerHTML` sets or retrieves the HTML content inside the element.

Question 4

To remove a node, you would use:

- A) `node.destroy()`
- B) `node.parentNode.removeChild(node)`

- C) `node.delete()`
- D) `node.removeChild(node)`

Answer: B) `node.parentNode.removeChild(node)`

Explanation: Removing a node requires calling `removeChild()` on the parent node. Alternatively, `node.remove()` can be used in modern browsers.

Question 5

Which method replaces one child node with another?
- A) `replaceChild(newNode, oldNode)`
- B) `swapChild(newNode, oldNode)`
- C) `changeChild(newNode, oldNode)`
- D) `updateChild(newNode, oldNode)`

Answer: A) `replaceChild(newNode, oldNode)`

Explanation: `replaceChild()` replaces an existing child with a new node.

Question 6

What does `document.createTextNode('Hello')` return?
- A) A string `'Hello'`
- B) A text node containing "Hello"
- C) A `<p>` element with "Hello"
- D) `undefined`

Answer: B) A text node containing "Hello"

Explanation: `createTextNode()` creates a text node, not an element.

Question 7

Which property should you use to safely insert user-generated text without HTML parsing?

- A) `element.innerHTML`
- B) `element.outerHTML`
- C) `element.textContent`
- D) `element.value`

Answer: C) `element.textContent`

Explanation: `textContent` sets text safely without parsing it as HTML.

Question 8

Which method creates a lightweight container to hold multiple nodes before attaching them to the DOM?
- A) `document.createDocumentFragment()`
- B) `document.createLightContainer()`
- C) `document.createBox()`
- D) `document.createVirtualNode()`

Answer: A) `document.createDocumentFragment()`

Explanation: DocumentFragments are used to improve performance when adding multiple nodes.

Question 9

`innerHTML` can pose a security risk if used with:
- A) Static content
- B) Secure, known HTML strings
- C) Unsanitized user input
- D) Empty strings

Answer: C) Unsanitized user input

Explanation: `innerHTML` can inject malicious code if used with unsanitized input.

Question 10

To insert a new node before a reference node, use:

- A) `insertBefore(newNode, referenceNode)`
- B) `appendChild(newNode, referenceNode)`
- C) `prependChild(newNode, referenceNode)`
- D) `insertNode(newNode, referenceNode)`

Answer: A) `insertBefore(newNode, referenceNode)`

Explanation: `insertBefore()` inserts a node before another specified child node.

Question 11

What does `cloneNode(true)` do?
- A) Returns a shallow clone of the node only.
- B) Returns a deep clone of the node and all descendants.
- C) Returns the node unchanged.
- D) Renames the node.

Answer: B) Returns a deep clone of the node and all descendants.

Explanation: Passing `true` to `cloneNode()` clones the entire subtree.

Question 12

Which of the following sets an attribute on an element?
- A)
`element.addAttribute('class','highlight')`
- B)
`element.setAttribute('class','highlight')`
- C) `element.attribute = 'class=highlight'`
- D) `element.setAttr('class','highlight')`

Answer: B)
`element.setAttribute('class','highlight')`

Explanation: `setAttribute()` is the correct method to set or change attributes.

Question 13

If you want to remove all children of an element `parent`, you can:
- A) `parent.innerHTML = ''`
- B) `parent.removeChild(parent)`
- C) `parent.setAttribute('children','')`
- D) `document.removeChild(parent)`

Answer: A) `parent.innerHTML = ''`

Explanation: Setting `innerHTML` to an empty string removes all child nodes. Although not the most efficient in all cases, it's a common approach.

Question 14

What is the main difference between `innerHTML` and `textContent`?
- A) `innerHTML` returns text only, `textContent` returns HTML.
- B) `innerHTML` can render HTML markup, `textContent` returns plain text.
- C) `textContent` can inject HTML, `innerHTML` cannot.
- D) They are identical in functionality.

Answer: B) `innerHTML` can render HTML markup, `textContent` returns plain text.

Explanation: `innerHTML` parses HTML, while `textContent` is just text.

Question 15

Which method can be used to remove a node directly, without referencing its parent?
- A) `node.remove()`
- B) `node.delete()`
- C) `node.cut()`
- D) `node.destroy()`

Answer: A) `node.remove()`

Explanation: Modern browsers support `remove()` on the element itself.

Question 16

To improve performance when adding 1000 items to a list:
- A) Use a DocumentFragment to append all items at once.
- B) Append items one by one using `appendChild()` directly to the DOM.
- C) Use `innerHTML` for each individual item.
- D) No difference in approach.

Answer: A) Use a DocumentFragment to append all items at once.

Explanation: DocumentFragments reduce reflows and improve performance.

Question 17

What does `parentNode` refer to?
- A) The element's child node.
- B) The element's parent node.
- C) Always the `<html>` element.
- D) The node's first sibling.

Answer: B) The element's parent node.

Explanation: `parentNode` returns the node's parent in the DOM tree.

Question 18

After creating a new element with `createElement()`, to display it on the page you must:
- A) Do nothing, it appears automatically.
- B) Call `renderElement()`.
- C) Append it to an existing element using `appendChild()` or similar methods.
- D) Use `document.write()`.

Answer: C) Append it to an existing element.

Explanation: Created elements are in memory and must be appended to the DOM.

Question 19

What does `element.style.color = 'red';` do?
- A) Changes the text color of `element` to red.
- B) Sets a new attribute `color` on the element.
- C) Inserts `<span style="color:red;">` inside the element.
- D) Removes the element's text.

Answer: A) Changes the text color of `element` to red.

Explanation: Accessing the `style` property sets inline CSS properties.

Question 20

Which method would you use to create a text node "Hello"?
- A) `document.createTextNode('Hello')`
- B) `document.createElement('Hello')`
- C) `document.innerText('Hello')`
- D) `document.createHTML('Hello')`

Answer: A) `document.createTextNode('Hello')`
Explanation: `createTextNode()` creates a text node.

10 Coding Exercises with Full Solutions

Exercise 1: Create and Append an Element

Task: Create a new `<p>` element with the text "Hello World" and append it to a `<div id="container">`.
HTML:
`<div id="container"></div>`
Solution:
```
const container =
document.getElementById('container');
const p = document.createElement('p');
p.textContent = 'Hello World';
container.appendChild(p);
```
Explanation:
We used `createElement` to make a `<p>` and `appendChild` to insert it.

Exercise 2: Insert Before Another Element

Task: Insert a new `<li>New Item</li>` before an existing `<li id="referenceItem"></li>` in a `<ul>`.
HTML:
```
<ul id="myList">
  <li>Item 1</li>
  <li id="referenceItem">Item 2</li>
  <li>Item 3</li>
</ul>
```
Solution:

```
const myList =
document.getElementById('myList');
const referenceItem =
document.getElementById('referenceItem');
const newLi = document.createElement('li');
newLi.textContent = 'New Item';
myList.insertBefore(newLi, referenceItem);
```
Explanation:
`insertBefore` places `newLi` before `referenceItem`.

Exercise 3: Replace an Element

Task: Replace a `<span id="oldSpan">` with a new
`<strong>New Content</strong>`.
HTML:
```
<div id="parentDiv">
  <span id="oldSpan">Old Content</span>
</div>
```
Solution:
```
const parentDiv =
document.getElementById('parentDiv');
const oldSpan =
document.getElementById('oldSpan');
const strong =
document.createElement('strong');
strong.textContent = 'New Content';
parentDiv.replaceChild(strong, oldSpan);
```
Explanation:
`replaceChild` swaps `oldSpan` with the new `strong`
element.

Exercise 4: Remove an Element

Task: Remove the element with `id="toRemove"` from the DOM.

HTML:

```
<div id="toRemove">Remove me!</div>
```

Solution:

```
const toRemove =
document.getElementById('toRemove');
toRemove.remove();
```

Explanation:

`remove()` directly removes the element from the DOM.

Exercise 5: Using innerHTML

Task: Set the inner HTML of a `<div id="content">` to `<h2>Title</h2><p>Paragraph</p>`.

HTML:

```
<div id="content"></div>
```

Solution:

```
const content =
document.getElementById('content');
content.innerHTML =
'<h2>Title</h2><p>Paragraph</p>';
```

Explanation:

`innerHTML` replaces the entire content of the element.

Exercise 6: Using textContent

Task: Change the text of a `<p id="text">` element to "Just Text" without parsing HTML.

HTML:

```
<p id="text"><strong>Bold text</strong></p>
```

Solution:

```
const textElem =
document.getElementById('text');
```

```
textElem.textContent = 'Just Text';
```
Explanation:
`textContent` removes any HTML formatting and sets plain text.

Exercise 7: Setting Attributes

Task: Create an `<a>` element, set its `href` to "https://example.com" and text to "Go to Example", then append it to `body`.
Solution:
```
const link = document.createElement('a');
link.setAttribute('href',
'https://example.com');
link.textContent = 'Go to Example';
document.body.appendChild(link);
```
Explanation:
`setAttribute` sets the `href` and we append it to the document.

Exercise 8: Using DocumentFragment

Task: Create a `DocumentFragment`, add 5 `<li>` elements with text "Item #", and then append the fragment to a `<ul id="list">`.
HTML:
```
<ul id="list"></ul>
```
Solution:
```
const fragment =
document.createDocumentFragment();
for (let i = 1; i <= 5; i++) {
  const li = document.createElement('li');
  li.textContent = 'Item ' + i;
```

```
    fragment.appendChild(li);
}
document.getElementById('list').appendChild
(fragment);
```
Explanation:
We build the list in a fragment, then append it all at once.

Exercise 9: Cloning an Element

Task: Clone an element with `id="original"` and
append the clone to `body`.
HTML:
```
<div id="original">Original Content</div>
```
Solution:
```
const original =
document.getElementById('original');
const clone = original.cloneNode(true);
document.body.appendChild(clone);
```
Explanation:
`cloneNode(true)` duplicates `original` and we append
the copy.

Exercise 10: Removing All Children

Task: Remove all child elements from a `<div`
`id="container">`.
HTML:
```
<div id="container">
  <p>Child 1</p>
  <p>Child 2</p>
</div>
```
Solution:
```
const containerDiv =
document.getElementById('container');
```

```
containerDiv.innerHTML = ''; // Clears all
children
```
Explanation:

Setting `innerHTML` to an empty string removes all child nodes.

Conclusion

You now have a solid understanding of how to create, insert, replace, and remove DOM elements. You learned how to handle text and HTML content, work with attributes, and improve performance using DocumentFragments. Armed with these skills, you can dynamically build and modify your webpages as users interact with them.

Introduction to Forms and Input Handling in JavaScript

What Are Forms?

In web development, **forms** are HTML structures that allow users to input and submit data to a server or handle it client-side. Forms typically include elements like text inputs, checkboxes, radio buttons, select menus, and textareas, along with a submit button.

The Role of JavaScript in Forms

JavaScript is often used with forms to:
1. **Validate User Input** before it's sent to a server.

2. **Dynamically Update and Manipulate Form Fields** based on user actions.
3. **Handle Form Submission** events to either prevent submission, submit data via AJAX, or provide real-time feedback to users.

Key Concepts

- **Accessing Form Elements**: In JavaScript, you can access form elements via `document.getElementById()`, `document.querySelector()`, or through the form's elements collection (`document.forms`).
- **Reading and Writing Input Values**: Form elements have properties like `.value` (for text inputs, select, textarea) to get and set their current value.
- **Event Handling**: Common events include:
  - `input` or `change` events: Triggered when the user modifies the value.
  - `submit` event: Triggered when the user attempts to submit the form.
  - `focus` and `blur` events: Triggered when elements gain or lose focus.
- **Validation**: Checking if the input meets certain criteria (e.g., required fields, email format, password strength).
- **Preventing Default Submission**: Using `event.preventDefault()` to stop the form from submitting and do custom handling.

Client-Side vs. Server-Side Validation

- **Client-Side Validation** (using JavaScript) provides immediate feedback to the user without sending data to the server.

- **Server-Side Validation** is crucial for security since client-side validation can be bypassed. However, having client-side validation enhances user experience.

Approaches to Handling Form Submissions

1. **Default Submission**: The form sends a request to the server and refreshes the page.
2. **Prevent Default and Use JavaScript**: Use `event.preventDefault()` on `submit` event, gather form data, and send it via `fetch()` or `XMLHttpRequest()` without reloading the page.
3. **Validation Before Submission**: Check all required fields, formats, and constraints before allowing the form to be sent.

Detailed Code Examples

Example 1: Accessing and Logging Form Input Values

```
<!DOCTYPE html>
<html>
<head><title>Form Example</title></head>
<body>
<form id="myForm">
  <label for="username">Username:</label>
  <input type="text" id="username"
name="username">
  <label for="age">Age:</label>
  <input type="number" id="age" name="age">
  <button type="submit">Submit</button>
```

```
</form>
<script>
  const form =
document.getElementById('myForm');
  form.addEventListener('submit',
function(e) {
    e.preventDefault(); // prevent page
refresh
    const username =
document.getElementById('username').value;
    const age =
document.getElementById('age').value;
    console.log(`Username: ${username},
Age: ${age}`);
  });
</script>
</body>
</html>
```

Explanation:

On form submission, we prevent the default behavior and log the input values to the console.

Example 2: Simple Client-Side Validation

```
<!DOCTYPE html>
<html>
<head><title>Validation
Example</title></head>
<body>
<form id="signupForm">
  <label>Email: <input type="email"
id="email" required></label>
```

```
  <label>Password: <input type="password"
id="password" required
minlength="6"></label>
  <button type="submit">Sign Up</button>
</form>
<script>
const form =
document.getElementById('signupForm');
form.addEventListener('submit', (e) => {
  if (!form.checkValidity()) {
    e.preventDefault(); // prevent form
from submitting
    alert("Please fill in all fields
correctly!");
  }
});
</script>
</body>
</html>
```

Explanation:
HTML5 attributes like `required`, `type="email"`, and
`minlength` provide basic validation. The
`checkValidity()` method checks if all constraints are
met. If not, we prevent submission and alert the user.

Example 3: Custom Validation with JavaScript

```
<!DOCTYPE html>
<html>
<head><title>Custom
Validation</title></head>
<body>
```

```
<form id="registerForm">
  <label>Username: <input type="text"
id="regUsername"></label>
  <label>Email: <input type="email"
id="regEmail"></label>
  <button type="submit">Register</button>
</form>
<script>
const form =
document.getElementById('registerForm');
form.addEventListener('submit', (e) => {
  e.preventDefault();
  const username =
document.getElementById('regUsername').valu
e.trim();
  const email =
document.getElementById('regEmail').value.t
rim();
  if (username.length < 3) {
    alert("Username must be at least 3
characters long.");
    return;
  }
  if (!/^\S+@\S+\.\S+$/.test(email)) {
    alert("Please provide a valid email
address.");
    return;
  }
  alert("Form is valid. Submitting...");
  // Perform AJAX submission or form action
here.
});
</script>
```

```
</body>
</html>
```

Explanation:

We do custom checks using regex for email and length checks for username. If validation fails, we show an alert; otherwise, we proceed.

Example 4: Live Feedback on Input

```
<!DOCTYPE html>
<html>
<head><title>Live Feedback</title></head>
<body>
<form>
  <label>Password: <input type="password"
id="livePassword"></label>
  <p id="feedback"></p>
</form>
<script>
const pwdInput =
document.getElementById('livePassword');
const feedback =
document.getElementById('feedback');
pwdInput.addEventListener('input', () => {
  const pwd = pwdInput.value;
  if (pwd.length < 6) {
    feedback.textContent = "Password too
short!";
    feedback.style.color = "red";
  } else {
    feedback.textContent = "Good password
length.";
```

```
      feedback.style.color = "green";
  }
});
</script>
</body>
</html>
```

Explanation:
We give instant feedback as the user types in the password.

Example 5: Preventing Default Submission and Using Fetch

```
<!DOCTYPE html>
<html>
<head><title>AJAX Submission</title></head>
<body>
<form id="contactForm">
  <label>Name: <input type="text"
name="name" required></label>
  <label>Message: <textarea name="message"
required></textarea></label>
  <button type="submit">Send</button>
</form>
<script>
const contactForm =
document.getElementById('contactForm');
contactForm.addEventListener('submit', (e)
=> {
  e.preventDefault();
  const formData = new
FormData(contactForm);
  fetch('/submit', {
```

```
    method: 'POST',
    body: formData
  })
  .then(response => response.text())
  .then(data => alert(`Server Response:
${data}`))
  .catch(err => console.error(err));
});
</script>
</body>
</html>
```

Explanation:

We gather form data with `FormData`, send it via `fetch()` to `/submit`, and handle the response asynchronously.

Multiple Choice Questions

1. What does `event.preventDefault()` do in a form submit handler?

A. Refreshes the page.

B. Prevents the form from submitting normally.

C. Submits the form twice.

D. Clears all form fields.

Answer: B.

Calling `preventDefault()` stops the browser's default action of submitting the form and reloading the page.

2. Which property would you use to get the value of a text input in JavaScript?

A. `.innerText`

B. `.textContent`

C. `.value`

D. `.text`

Answer: C.

For form inputs, `.value` is used to read and modify the input's content.

3. **Which event is typically used to trigger form validation before submission?**

A. `click`

B. `submit`

C. `change`

D. `focus`

Answer: B.

The `submit` event is fired when the user attempts to submit the form, making it ideal for last-minute validation.

4. **What is `checkValidity()` used for?**

A. To check if form fields meet HTML5 validation constraints.

B. To remove all event listeners.

C. To make the form read-only.

D. To reset the form fields to default.

Answer: A.

`form.checkValidity()` returns true if all form controls meet their constraints, false otherwise.

5. **Which method is most appropriate to gather all input values at once before an AJAX request?**

A. `new FormData(formElement)`

B. `JSON.parse()`

C. `localStorage.getItem()`

D. `document.write()`

Answer: A.

`FormData` is a convenient API to collect form field values for AJAX submissions.

6. **Client-side validation is important because:**

A. It replaces server-side validation entirely.

B. It improves user experience by giving immediate

feedback.

C. It ensures no security issues remain.

D. It is mandatory for all forms to work.

Answer: B.

Client-side validation provides quick feedback, but server-side validation is still needed for security.

7. **To prevent a form from submitting if certain conditions aren't met, you can:**

A. Remove the `action` attribute.

B. Use `event.preventDefault()` in the `submit` event handler.

C. Hide the submit button.

D. None of the above.

Answer: B.

`preventDefault()` stops the normal submission, allowing you to validate first.

8. **Which HTML attribute is used to specify that an input field must be filled out before submitting?**

A. `required`

B. `min`

C. `pattern`

D. `checked`

Answer: A.

The `required` attribute ensures that the field cannot be left blank when submitting.

9. **If you want to provide real-time feedback as the user types, you should listen to which event?**

A. `submit`

B. `input`

C. `change`

D. `reset`

Answer: B.

The `input` event fires every time the value of the element changes, providing real-time feedback.

10. **Which method sends form data without refreshing the page?**

A. A standard form submit.

B. `fetch()` or `XMLHttpRequest()` with `FormData`.

C. `document.write()`

D. `alert()`

Answer: B.

Using `fetch()` or `XMLHttpRequest()` with `FormData` allows for AJAX submission without a page reload.

11. **What does the `pattern` attribute on an input do?**

A. It specifies a regular expression the input's value must match.

B. It changes the input's background color.

C. It sets a placeholder.

D. It encrypts the input.

Answer: A.

The `pattern` attribute uses a regex to validate the field's value.

12. **How do you stop form submission from reloading the page?**

A. By setting `form.action = " "`.

B. Using `event.preventDefault()` in the submit event handler.

C. Putting the form inside a `<div>`.

D. Removing the submit button.

Answer: B.

`preventDefault()` stops the default submission and page reload.

13. **Which is NOT a built-in HTML5 validation attribute?**

A. `required`

B. `maxlength`

C. `pattern`

D. `validateUrl`

Answer: D.

`validateUrl` is not a standard HTML5 form validation attribute.

14.   **To access a form element by name, you can use:**

A.

`document.forms["formName"].elements["elemen tName"]`

B. `document.getElementByClassName()`

C. `window.alert()`

D. `document.title`

Answer: A.

The `document.forms` collection allows access to form and its elements by name.

15.   **What does the `focus()` method do on a form element?**

A. Highlights the element.

B. Sets the keyboard focus to that element.

C. Submits the form.

D. Clears the input value.

Answer: B.

`focus()` sets the keyboard input focus to the element.

16.   **`blur()` event occurs when:**

A. The element gets focus.

B. The element loses focus.

C. The form is submitted.

D. The page loads.

Answer: B.

`blur()` fires when the element loses focus.

17.   **Which attribute prevents form submission when an input doesn't match the required pattern?**

A. `data-validate`
B. `pattern`
C. `no-submit`
D. `oninvalid`
Answer: B.
The `pattern` attribute will cause the browser's HTML5 validation to fail if the input doesn't match.
18. **To reset a form to its initial values, you can call:**
A. `form.reset()`
B. `form.clear()`
C. `form.delete()`
D. `form.refresh()`
Answer: A.
`form.reset()` resets the form to its initial state.
19. **For a `<select>` element, the chosen option's value is accessed by:**
A. `select.text`
B. `select.value`
C. `select.content`
D. `select.innerHTML`
Answer: B.
The currently selected option's value is given by `select.value`.
20. **To show a custom validation message, you can use:**
A. `input.setCustomValidity("message")`
B. `alert("message")` only
C. `input.customMessage = "message"`
D. `document.write("message")`
Answer: A.
`setCustomValidity()` sets a custom validation message that appears when validation fails.

10 Coding Exercises with Full Solutions and Explanations

Exercise 1: Display Input Value on Button Click

Task: Create an HTML form with a text input and a button. When the button is clicked, display the input's current value in a <p> element.

Solution:

```
<!DOCTYPE html>
<html>
<body>
  <input type="text" id="inputText">
  <button id="showBtn">Show Value</button>
  <p id="display"></p>
  <script>
    const inputText =
document.getElementById('inputText');
    const showBtn =
document.getElementById('showBtn');
    const display =
document.getElementById('display');
    showBtn.addEventListener('click', () =>
{
      display.textContent =
inputText.value;
    });
  </script>
</body>
</html>
```

Explanation:
We use a button click event to set
`display.textContent` to the input's `.value`.

Exercise 2: Prevent Form Submission if Field is Empty

Task: Create a form with a required text input. If the input is empty, show an alert and prevent submission.
Solution:

```
<!DOCTYPE html>
<html>
<body>
<form id="myForm">
  <input type="text" id="requiredField"
placeholder="Type something" required>
  <button type="submit">Submit</button>
</form>
<script>
const form =
document.getElementById('myForm');
form.addEventListener('submit', (e) => {
  const value =
document.getElementById('requiredField').va
lue.trim();
  if (value === '') {
    e.preventDefault();
    alert("Field cannot be empty!");
  }
});
</script>
</body>
</html>
```

Explanation:

If the field is empty, `preventDefault()` stops submission and alerts the user.

Exercise 3: Real-Time Email Validation Using Regex

Task: Add an email input. As the user types, check if it's a valid email format. Show a green message if valid, red if not.

Solution:

```
<!DOCTYPE html>
<html>
<body>
<input type="email" id="emailInput"
placeholder="Enter email">
<p id="emailFeedback"></p>
<script>
const emailInput =
document.getElementById('emailInput');
const emailFeedback =
document.getElementById('emailFeedback');
emailInput.addEventListener('input', () =>
{
  const email = emailInput.value;
  const isValid =
/^\S+@\S+\.\S+$/.test(email);
  if (isValid) {
    emailFeedback.textContent = "Valid
email!";
    emailFeedback.style.color = "green";
  } else {
```

```
    emailFeedback.textContent = "Invalid
email!";
    emailFeedback.style.color = "red";
  }
});
</script>
</body>
</html>
```
Explanation:
We use a regex and the `input` event to give immediate feedback.

Exercise 4: Toggle Password Visibility

Task: Create a password input and a checkbox. When the checkbox is checked, show the password in plain text; otherwise, hide it.
Solution:
```
<!DOCTYPE html>
<html>
<body>
<label>Password:
  <input type="password"
id="passwordField">
</label>
<label>Show Password
  <input type="checkbox"
id="toggleCheckbox">
</label>
<script>
const passwordField =
document.getElementById('passwordField');
```

```javascript
const toggleCheckbox =
document.getElementById('toggleCheckbox');
toggleCheckbox.addEventListener('change',
() => {
  passwordField.type =
toggleCheckbox.checked ? "text" :
"password";
});
</script>
</body>
</html>
```

Explanation:

By changing the type attribute, we toggle between hidden and visible password.

Exercise 5: Dynamic Select Options

Task: Have a select element and a text input. When the user types a new option name and presses "Add Option," add that option to the select dropdown.

Solution:

```html
<!DOCTYPE html>
<html>
<body>
<select id="mySelect">
  <option value="default">Default
Option</option>
</select>
<input type="text" id="newOption"
placeholder="New option name">
<button id="addOptionBtn">Add
Option</button>
```

```
<script>
const mySelect =
document.getElementById('mySelect');
const newOption =
document.getElementById('newOption');
const addOptionBtn =
document.getElementById('addOptionBtn');
addOptionBtn.addEventListener('click', ()
=> {
  const val = newOption.value.trim();
  if (val) {
    const option =
document.createElement('option');
    option.value = val;
    option.textContent = val;
    mySelect.appendChild(option);
    newOption.value = '';
  }
});
</script>
</body>
</html>
```

Explanation:
We create a new `<option>` element dynamically and append it to the select.

Exercise 6: Character Count for Textarea

Task: Create a textarea and a p element that shows how many characters have been typed out of a max limit (e.g., 100 chars).
Solution:
```
<!DOCTYPE html>
```

```
<html>
<body>
<textarea id="myTextArea"
maxlength="100"></textarea>
<p id="charCount"></p>
<script>
const myTextArea =
document.getElementById('myTextArea');
const charCount =
document.getElementById('charCount');
myTextArea.addEventListener('input', () =>
{
  const length = myTextArea.value.length;
  charCount.textContent = `${length}/100
characters`;
});
</script>
</body>
</html>
```

Explanation:
The input event updates the character count display as the user types.

Exercise 7: Submit Form Data via Fetch and Display Response

Task: On form submit, prevent default, send data to a mock endpoint using fetch, and display the server response in a p element.
Solution:
```
<!DOCTYPE html>
<html>
```

```html
<body>
<form id="dataForm">
  <input type="text" name="username"
required placeholder="Username">
  <button type="submit">Send</button>
</form>
<p id="responseText"></p>
<script>
const dataForm =
document.getElementById('dataForm');
const responseText =
document.getElementById('responseText');
dataForm.addEventListener('submit', (e) =>
{
  e.preventDefault();
  const formData = new FormData(dataForm);
  fetch('https://example.com/submit', {
    method: 'POST',
    body: formData
  })
  .then(resp => resp.text())
  .then(data => {
    responseText.textContent = `Server
Response: ${data}`;
  })
  .catch(err => console.error(err));
});
</script>
</body>
</html>
```

Explanation:
We simulate sending data to example.com, then update responseText with the response.

Exercise 8: Form Reset Button

Task: Create a form with several inputs and a reset button. When the reset button is clicked, all fields should return to their initial values.

Solution:

```
<!DOCTYPE html>
<html>
<body>
<form id="exampleForm">
  <input type="text" name="firstName"
value="John">
  <input type="number" name="age"
value="30">
  <button type="reset">Reset</button>
</form>
</body>
</html>
```

Explanation:

The `reset` button automatically calls `form.reset()` which restores initial values.

Exercise 9: Validate On Blur

Task: Validate a required email input when it loses focus. If invalid, show a red border, else show a green border.

Solution:

```
<!DOCTYPE html>
<html>
<body>
<input type="email" id="blurEmail"
placeholder="Enter email">
```

```
<script>
const blurEmail =
document.getElementById('blurEmail');
blurEmail.addEventListener('blur', () => {
  const value = blurEmail.value.trim();
  if (/^\S+@\S+\.\S+$/.test(value)) {
    blurEmail.style.borderColor = "green";
  } else {
    blurEmail.style.borderColor = "red";
  }
});
</script>
</body>
</html>
```

Explanation:
On blur, we check validity. If invalid, highlight with red border.

Exercise 10: Disable Submit Until Checked

Task: Create a checkbox with the label "I agree to terms". The submit button should be disabled until the checkbox is checked.
Solution:
```
<!DOCTYPE html>
<html>
<body>
<form>
  <label><input type="checkbox"
id="termsCheck"> I agree to terms</label>
  <button id="submitBtn" type="submit"
disabled>Submit</button>
</form>
```

```
<script>
const termsCheck =
document.getElementById('termsCheck');
const submitBtn =
document.getElementById('submitBtn');
termsCheck.addEventListener('change', () =>
{
  submitBtn.disabled = !termsCheck.checked;
});
</script>
</body>
</html>
```

Explanation:
We toggle the `disabled` property of the submit button based on the checkbox's state.

Conclusion

Handling forms and user inputs in JavaScript involves understanding how to access form elements, read and write their values, validate inputs, provide real-time feedback, and control the submission process. By combining HTML5 built-in validation attributes with JavaScript event handling, regex checks, and AJAX submissions using `fetch()`, developers can create a robust and user-friendly form experience.

JavaScript: Browser Storage (localStorage, sessionStorage, and cookies)

Browser storage APIs allow you to store data on the client-side and persist it across page reloads, sessions, or until manually cleared. Understanding how to use **localStorage**, **sessionStorage**, and **cookies** is crucial for building feature-rich, stateful web applications without always relying on server-side persistence.

Introduction to Browser Storage

Modern web browsers provide several storage mechanisms for persisting data on the client-side:
- **localStorage**: Stores data with no expiration date, tied to the domain.
- **sessionStorage**: Stores data for one browser session. Data is cleared when the browser tab is closed.
- **Cookies**: Older mechanism, sent with every HTTP request, configurable expiration, size limits, and can be used for session tracking.

Storing data client-side can reduce the need for server round-trips, improve performance, and maintain state across pages.

localStorage

localStorage is a key-value storage that persists even after the browser is closed and reopened (until cleared manually or programmatically).

Key Points:
- Data is stored per domain and protocol.
- Stored data is accessible from any page under the same domain.
- Data is stored indefinitely until cleared by user or code.
- Storage limit is typically around 5MB.

Common Methods:
- `localStorage.setItem(key, value)`
- `localStorage.getItem(key)`
- `localStorage.removeItem(key)`
- `localStorage.clear()` (Removes all entries)
- `localStorage.key(index)` (Get key by index)

Example:
```
// Store data
localStorage.setItem('username',
'JohnDoe');
// Retrieve data
const user =
localStorage.getItem('username'); //
'JohnDoe'
// Remove data
localStorage.removeItem('username');
// Clear all data
localStorage.clear();
```

sessionStorage

sessionStorage works similar to localStorage but is limited to a single browser tab/session.

Key Points:

- Data is kept only for the duration of the page session.
- Once the tab is closed, data is lost.
- Methods are the same as localStorage.

Example:

```
// Store data for this session
sessionStorage.setItem('sessionID',
'abc123');
// Retrieve it
const sessionID =
sessionStorage.getItem('sessionID'); //
'abc123'
// Remove it
sessionStorage.removeItem('sessionID');
// Clear all session data
sessionStorage.clear();
```

Cookies

Cookies are small pieces of data stored in key-value pairs. They are sent to the server with every HTTP request.

Key Points:

- Typically limited to around 4KB of data per cookie.
- Set with an expiration date or they become session cookies.
- Accessible via `document.cookie`.
- Must be manually serialized, as `document.cookie` is a single string.
- Cookies can specify `path`, `domain`, `secure`, `SameSite` attributes for security and scope.

Setting a Cookie:

```javascript
// Set a cookie valid for 7 days
const date = new Date();
date.setDate(date.getDate() + 7);
document.cookie = `username=JohnDoe;
expires=${date.toUTCString()}; path=/`;
```

Reading Cookies:

```javascript
// document.cookie returns all cookies in a
single string
// Example: "username=JohnDoe; theme=dark"
const allCookies = document.cookie;
// To get a specific cookie, parse the
string
function getCookie(name) {
  const match =
document.cookie.match('(^|;)\\s*' + name +
'=([^;]+)');
  return match ? match[2] : null;
}
console.log(getCookie('username')); //
'JohnDoe'
```

Deleting a Cookie:

```javascript
// To delete a cookie, set an expiration
date in the past
document.cookie = 'username=; expires=Thu,
01 Jan 1970 00:00:00 UTC; path=/;';
```

Choosing the Right Storage Mechanism

- **localStorage**: Best for storing large amounts of key-value data that you want to persist across sessions.

- **sessionStorage**: Ideal for temporary data that only matters for a single browser session/tab.
- **Cookies**: Useful for server-side sessions, small amounts of data that need to be sent to the server, or legacy support. Also for cross-tab data if needed by the server.

Consider:
- Data size limits.
- Security and sensitivity of stored data.
- Need for expiration or session-based clearing.
- Whether data should be available to the server.

Security Considerations

- All these storage mechanisms are accessible from client-side JavaScript, meaning sensitive data can be exposed if the site is compromised.
- Avoid storing highly sensitive information (like passwords, tokens) in plain text.
- Use secure flags and `SameSite` attributes for cookies.
- Consider encryption or server validation for tokens.

Multiple Choice Questions

Question 1

Which storage mechanism persists even after the browser is closed and reopened?
- A) sessionStorage
- B) localStorage
- C) Cookies (with no expiration)
- D) None of the above

Answer: B) localStorage
Explanation: localStorage data persists until manually cleared.

Question 2

Which storage is cleared when the browser tab is closed?
- A) localStorage
- B) sessionStorage
- C) Cookies
- D) IndexedDB

Answer: B) sessionStorage
Explanation: sessionStorage is unique to each tab and is cleared when the tab is closed.

Question 3

How would you store a value with localStorage?
- A) `document.setLocalItem('key','value')`
- B) `localStorage.setItem('key','value')`
- C) `localStorage.save('key','value')`
- D) `window.setItem('key','value')`

Answer: B) `localStorage.setItem('key','value')`

Question 4

What is the typical size limit of localStorage?
- A) About 5MB per domain
- B) About 4KB total
- C) Unlimited
- D) Exactly 1MB

Answer: A) About 5MB per domain

Question 5

Which method removes a single item from localStorage?
- A) `localStorage.clearItem('key')`
- B) `localStorage.deleteItem('key')`
- C) `localStorage.removeItem('key')`
- D) `localStorage.dropItem('key')`

Answer: C) `localStorage.removeItem('key')`

Question 6

To remove all items from localStorage:
- A) `localStorage.clear()`
- B) `localStorage.removeAll()`
- C) `localStorage.flush()`
- D) `localStorage = {}`

Answer: A) `localStorage.clear()`

Question 7

sessionStorage differs from localStorage mainly because:
- A) sessionStorage data never expires.
- B) sessionStorage data is cleared on tab close.
- C) sessionStorage can store larger data than localStorage.
- D) sessionStorage is shared across all browser tabs.

Answer: B) sessionStorage data is cleared on tab close.

Question 8

Which of the following is a correct way to set a cookie?
- A) `cookies.username = "JohnDoe";`
- B) `document.cookie = "username=JohnDoe";`
- C) `localStorage.cookie = "username=JohnDoe";`
- D) `setCookie("username", "JohnDoe");`

Answer: B) `document.cookie =
"username=JohnDoe";`

Question 9

Cookies are automatically sent to the server with:
- A) Every XMLHttpRequest
- B) Every HTTP request
- C) Only POST requests
- D) Only secure requests

Answer: B) Every HTTP request

Explanation: Cookies are included in the HTTP headers sent to the server.

Question 10

To make a cookie expire after 7 days, you must set:
- A) `expires` attribute
- B) `session` attribute
- C) `timeout` attribute
- D) `expiry` attribute

Answer: A) `expires` attribute

Explanation: The `expires` or `max-age` attribute controls the cookie expiration.

Question 11

The maximum size of a cookie is typically around:
- A) 4KB
- B) 5MB
- C) 10MB
- D) 1GB

Answer: A) 4KB

Question 12

Which storage method is best for persisting large amounts of user preferences?
- A) Cookies
- B) localStorage
- C) sessionStorage
- D) window.name

Answer: B) localStorage

Explanation: localStorage can store more data than cookies and persists indefinitely.

Question 13

To remove a cookie, you must:
- A) Delete it from localStorage
- B) Use `removeCookie('name')`
- C) Set the cookie again with an expiration date in the past
- D) sessionStorage.clear()

Answer: C) Set the cookie with an expiration in the past

Question 14

If you want data to be available only for the current tab's lifetime, use:
- A) localStorage
- B) sessionStorage
- C) Cookies with expiry in the past
- D) Cookies with `session` flag

Answer: B) sessionStorage

Question 15

Are cookies accessible from JavaScript by default?

- A) Yes, all cookies are always accessible.
- B) No, cookies are HTTP-only by default.
- C) Depends on the `HttpOnly` attribute.
- D) Only if `secure` is set.

Answer: C) Depends on the `HttpOnly` attribute.

Explanation: If `HttpOnly` is set, cookies are not accessible by JavaScript.

Question 16

To store a JSON object in localStorage, you should:
- A) Just assign the object:
`localStorage.setItem('obj', {a:1});`
- B) Convert to JSON string first:
`localStorage.setItem('obj',`
`JSON.stringify({a:1}));`
- C) Convert to Base64
- D) Use `localStorage.setJson('obj',{a:1});`

Answer: B) Convert to JSON string first

Explanation: localStorage only stores strings.

Question 17

When would you prefer cookies over localStorage?
- A) To store large amounts of data that never expire.
- B) To store session tokens that the server needs.
- C) To store temporary data for one tab session.
- D) Never, cookies are outdated.

Answer: B) To store session tokens that the server needs.

Explanation: Cookies are sent to the server with requests, useful for auth tokens.

Question 18

Which storage does not send data to the server automatically?

- A) Cookies
- B) localStorage
- C) Both send data
- D) None

Answer: B) localStorage

Explanation: localStorage data is not sent with HTTP requests.

Question 19

To retrieve an item from localStorage:

- A) `localStorage.get('key')`
- B) `localStorage.fetch('key')`
- C) `localStorage.getItem('key')`
- D) `localStorage.query('key')`

Answer: C) `localStorage.getItem('key')`

Question 20

`sessionStorage` is cleared when:

- A) The browser is closed
- B) The tab or window is closed
- C) The user logs out
- D) The user clears browsing data

Answer: B) The tab or window is closed

Explanation: sessionStorage is tied to a single browsing session/tab.

10 Coding Exercises with Full Solutions and Explanations

Exercise 1: Store and Retrieve LocalStorage Item

Task: Store a user's name ("`Alice`") in localStorage under the key "`username`" and then log it.
Solution:
```
localStorage.setItem('username', 'Alice');
console.log(localStorage.getItem('username'
)); // "Alice"
```
Explanation:
We use `setItem` and then `getItem` to store and retrieve a value.

Exercise 2: Remove an Item from localStorage

Task: Remove the "`username`" item from localStorage.
Solution:
```
localStorage.removeItem('username');
```
Explanation:
`removeItem` deletes a specific key-value pair from localStorage.

Exercise 3: Clear All localStorage

Task: Clear all entries in localStorage.
Solution:
```
localStorage.clear();
```
Explanation:
`clear()` wipes out all stored data in localStorage for the current domain.

Exercise 4: Using sessionStorage

Task: Store a `"sessionID"` in sessionStorage and then retrieve it.
Solution:
```
sessionStorage.setItem('sessionID',
'xyz123');
console.log(sessionStorage.getItem('session
ID')); // "xyz123"
```
Explanation:
sessionStorage methods are identical to localStorage methods.

Exercise 5: Storing a JSON Object in localStorage

Task: Store a user object `{ name: "Bob", age: 25 }` in localStorage.
Solution:
```
const user = { name: 'Bob', age: 25 };
localStorage.setItem('user',
JSON.stringify(user));
// Retrieve
const storedUser =
JSON.parse(localStorage.getItem('user'));
console.log(storedUser.name); // "Bob"
```
Explanation:
Convert objects to JSON strings before storing, and parse when retrieving.

Exercise 6: Set a Cookie

Task: Set a cookie named `"color"` with the value `"blue"` that expires in 7 days.
Solution:
```
function setCookie(name, value, days) {
  const date = new Date();
```

```
  date.setTime(date.getTime() +
(days*24*60*60*1000));
  const expires = "expires="+
date.toUTCString();
  document.cookie = name + "=" + value +
";" + expires + ";path=/";
}
setCookie('color', 'blue', 7);
```
Explanation:
We set `expires` and `path` to make a persistent cookie.

Exercise 7: Get a Cookie Value

Task: Retrieve the value of `"color"` cookie set in the previous exercise.
Solution:
```
function getCookie(name) {
  const match =
document.cookie.match('(^|;)\\s*' + name +
'=([^;]+)');
  return match ? match[2] : null;
}
console.log(getCookie('color')); // "blue"
```
Explanation:
We use a regex to parse `document.cookie` string.

Exercise 8: Delete a Cookie

Task: Delete the `"color"` cookie.
Solution:
```
document.cookie = "color=; expires=Thu, 01
Jan 1970 00:00:00 UTC; path=/;";
```

Explanation:
Setting the cookie's expiration to a past date removes it.

Exercise 9: Check if localStorage Key Exists

Task: Check if `"theme"` key exists in localStorage. If not, set it to `"light"`.
Solution:
```
if (!localStorage.getItem('theme')) {
  localStorage.setItem('theme', 'light');
}
```
Explanation:
`getItem` returns `null` if the key doesn't exist.

Exercise 10: Temporary Data with sessionStorage

Task: On page load, increment a `"visitCount"` in sessionStorage and log it.
Solution:
```
let visitCount =
sessionStorage.getItem('visitCount');
visitCount = visitCount ?
parseInt(visitCount, 10) + 1 : 1;
sessionStorage.setItem('visitCount',
visitCount);
console.log('This is your visit number:',
visitCount);
```
Explanation:
If `visitCount` doesn't exist, start at 1; otherwise increment. The data resets when the tab is closed.

Conclusion

By mastering localStorage, sessionStorage, and cookies, you can effectively handle client-side persistence. Choose the right mechanism based on the longevity and scope of your data. Remember to consider security and performance implications, and always treat client-side data as potentially tampered with. With these tools at your disposal, you can build more responsive and stateful web applications.

JavaScript: Custom Events (dispatchEvent, CustomEvent, and Event-Driven Programming)

Custom events in JavaScript allow you to create and emit your own events, making it possible to decouple different parts of your application and enable event-driven architecture. This can improve code organization, reusability, and the ability to react to various application states and interactions.

Introduction to Event-Driven Programming

Event-driven programming is a paradigm in which the flow of the program is determined by events—user actions like clicks or key presses, system-generated events, or custom-defined events. Rather than constantly checking for conditions, your code can "listen" for events and respond accordingly. This leads to cleaner, more modular code, since components can react to events rather than being tightly coupled.

What are Custom Events?

Custom events are user-defined events that you can create and dispatch on DOM elements (or the `window` object) to signal that something has happened in your code. Instead of relying solely on standard browser events (`click`, `load`, `submit`), you can create events like "`data-loaded`", "`user-logged-in`", or "`modal-opened`". For example, you could dispatch a custom event when you finish loading data from an API. Another component listening for that event can then update the UI accordingly.

The Event Constructor and CustomEvent

The `Event` constructor and `CustomEvent` constructor allow you to create event objects:

- **new `Event(type, options)`**: Creates a basic event.
- **new `CustomEvent(type, { detail: ... })`**: Creates a custom event with additional data in the `detail` property.

Example using CustomEvent:

```
const myEvent = new CustomEvent('my-custom-
event', {
  detail: { message: 'Hello World!' },
  bubbles: true,
  cancelable: true,
});
```

This creates an event named `'my-custom-event'` that bubbles up the DOM and can be canceled, and includes extra data under `detail`.

Dispatching Custom Events

To trigger a custom event, you use `element.dispatchEvent(event)` on a DOM node. The event will then travel through the DOM (if bubbles is true) and invoke any event listeners that match its event type.

Example:

```
const button =
document.getElementById('myButton');
const customEvent = new
CustomEvent('greet', {
  detail: { name: 'Alice' }
});
button.dispatchEvent(customEvent);
```

This dispatches the `'greet'` event on `button`.

Listening for Custom Events

To listen for a custom event, use `addEventListener` on the target element (or its ancestors, if the event bubbles).

```
button.addEventListener('greet', (event) =>
{
  console.log('Greet event received:',
event.detail.name);
});
```

When the `'greet'` event is dispatched, the listener will run and log the name.

Passing Data with Custom Events

One of the biggest advantages of `CustomEvent` is the `detail` property. It allows you to attach any object or value to the event, so that the listener can access additional context.

Example:

```
const dataLoadedEvent = new
CustomEvent('data-loaded', {
  detail: { items: [1, 2, 3], timestamp:
Date.now() }
});
// Dispatch on a global object, like
document
document.dispatchEvent(dataLoadedEvent);
document.addEventListener('data-loaded',
(e) => {
  console.log('Data Loaded:',
e.detail.items);
});
```

Practical Use Cases

- **Module Communication**: Different parts of your app can communicate without direct references.
- **Decoupling Components**: A data fetching module can dispatch a 'data-ready' event, and UI components can react accordingly.

- **Plugin Architecture**: Custom events are useful when building plugins that need to integrate with host pages.
- **State Changes**: Signal application state changes (like user login, logout).

Multiple Choice Questions

Question 1

Which constructor is used to create events that include a `detail` object?
- A) `new Event()`
- B) `new CustomEvent()`
- C) `new DetailEvent()`
- D) `new EventObject()`

Answer: B) `new CustomEvent()`

Explanation: `CustomEvent` allows setting a `detail` property for additional data.

Question 2

How do you dispatch a custom event?
- A) `element.fireEvent(event)`
- B) `element.triggerEvent(event)`
- C) `element.dispatchEvent(event)`
- D) `document.createEvent('event')`

Answer: C) `element.dispatchEvent(event)`

Explanation: `dispatchEvent` is the standard method to fire an event on an element.

Question 3

What property of `CustomEvent` is used to pass additional data?

- A) `event.extra`
- B) `event.data`
- C) `event.detail`
- D) `event.payload`

Answer: C) `event.detail`

Explanation: The `detail` property is where custom event data is stored.

Question 4

How do you listen for a custom event `myEvent` on document?

- A) `document.onMyEvent = function(){}`
- B) `document.addEventListener('myEvent', callback)`
- C) `document.listen('myEvent', callback)`
- D) `document.addCustomEventListener('myEvent', callback)`

Answer: B) `document.addEventListener('myEvent', callback)`

Explanation: `addEventListener` is used for all events, including custom ones.

Question 5

Which of these is NOT true about custom events?

- A) They can bubble if configured.
- B) They can carry extra data via `detail`.
- C) They are part of the DOM event model.
- D) They are automatically dispatched on page load.

Answer: D) They are automatically dispatched on page load.

Explanation: Custom events are dispatched only when you explicitly call `dispatchEvent`.

Question 6

To prevent an event from bubbling up the DOM, you use:
- A) `event.preventDefault()`
- B) `event.stopPropagation()`
- C) `event.cancelBubble = true`
- D) `event.preventBubble()`

Answer: B) `event.stopPropagation()`

Explanation: `stopPropagation()` stops the event from reaching higher-level elements.

Question 7

Which option in `CustomEvent` constructor sets whether the event bubbles?
- A) `bubbles: true`
- B) `cancelable: true`
- C) `composed: true`
- D) `propagate: true`

Answer: A) `bubbles: true`

Explanation: The `bubbles` property controls event bubbling.

Question 8

`dispatchEvent` returns:
- A) `true` if the event was not canceled, otherwise `false`
- B) The event object

- C) The detail data
- D) Nothing

Answer: A) `true` if not canceled, otherwise `false`

Explanation: `dispatchEvent()` returns a boolean indicating whether `preventDefault()` was called by a listener.

Question 9

Which method is used to create a generic event without `detail`?
- A) `new Event('type')`
- B) `createGenericEvent('type')`
- C) `new BasicEvent('type')`
- D) `Event('type', {detail:{}})`

Answer: A) `new Event('type')`

Explanation: The `Event` constructor creates a standard event with no detail property.

Question 10

Can custom events be canceled?
- A) Yes, if `cancelable: true` was set.
- B) No, custom events cannot be canceled.
- C) Only if using `Event` not `CustomEvent`.
- D) Only if the event name starts with `"cancel-"`.

Answer: A) Yes, if `cancelable: true` was set.

Explanation: Setting `cancelable` allows calling `event.preventDefault()`.

Question 11

What is the main difference between `Event` and `CustomEvent`?

- A) `CustomEvent` can include `detail` data.
- B) `Event` can bubble, `CustomEvent` cannot.
- C) `Event` is only for native events.
- D) `CustomEvent` does not work in modern browsers.

Answer: A) `CustomEvent` can include `detail` data.

Explanation: `CustomEvent` adds the `detail` property for extra info.

Question 12

To attach multiple event listeners to the same custom event:
- A) Only one listener can be added per event type.
- B) Add multiple `addEventListener` calls.
- C) You must use `CustomEvent()` for multiple listeners.
- D) Use `event.addMultipleListeners()`.

Answer: B) Add multiple `addEventListener` calls.

Explanation: Just call `addEventListener` multiple times with different callbacks.

Question 13

When might you use a custom event?
- A) To replace a `click` event
- B) To signal completion of a data fetch
- C) To trigger the browser's built-in history navigation
- D) To read a file from disk

Answer: B) To signal completion of a data fetch

Explanation: Custom events are great for signaling state changes or asynchronous completions.

Question 14

If `bubbles` is set to false:
- A) The event does not propagate upward.
- B) The event cannot be canceled.
- C) The event detail is removed.
- D) The event fires twice.

Answer: A) The event does not propagate upward.
Explanation: Without bubbling, the event stays on the dispatched element.

Question 15

`CustomEvent` was introduced to:
- A) Deprecate `Event`
- B) Provide a standard way to pass custom data with events
- C) Only for debugging
- D) Only for touch events

Answer: B) Provide a standard way to pass custom data with events
Explanation: `CustomEvent` allows custom data and a standardized approach.

Question 16

If you call `event.preventDefault()` on a non-cancelable event:
- A) It throws an error.
- B) It does nothing.
- C) It cancels the event anyway.
- D) It changes `detail` to null.

Answer: B) It does nothing.
Explanation: `preventDefault()` has no effect if the event is not cancelable.

Question 17

Which property holds the event name?
- A) `event.detail`
- B) `event.name`
- C) `event.type`
- D) `event.eventName`

Answer: C) `event.type`

Explanation: `type` property gives the event type string.

Question 18

Can you dispatch a custom event from `window`?
- A) No, only from DOM elements.
- B) Yes, you can dispatch from `window`, `document`, or any DOM element.
- C) Only if `CustomEvent` was not used.
- D) Only if `bubbles: true`.

Answer: B) Yes, you can dispatch from `window`, `document`, or any DOM element.

Explanation: Any EventTarget, including `window` and `document`, supports dispatchEvent.

Question 19

What does `event.currentTarget` refer to?
- A) The element that added the event listener.
- B) The element that dispatched the event.
- C) The element clicked by the user.
- D) The global object.

Answer: A) The element that added the event listener.

Explanation: `currentTarget` is the element whose listener is running.

Question 20

To stop the event from being heard by other listeners at the same level:

- A) `event.stopPropagation()`
- B) `event.stopImmediatePropagation()`
- C) `event.preventDefault()`
- D) `event.halt()`

Answer: B) `event.stopImmediatePropagation()`
Explanation: `stopImmediatePropagation()` stops other listeners on the same element.

10 Coding Exercises with Full Solutions

Exercise 1: Create and Dispatch a Simple Custom Event

Task: Create a `CustomEvent` named `"greet"` with a detail of `{ name: "Alice" }`, dispatch it on `document`, and log the detail in a listener.
Solution:

```
// Listener
document.addEventListener('greet', (event)
=> {
  console.log('Greet event received:',
event.detail.name); // "Alice"
});
// Create and dispatch
const greetEvent = new CustomEvent('greet',
{
  detail: { name: 'Alice' }
});
document.dispatchEvent(greetEvent);
```

Explanation:
We first set up a listener, then create a `CustomEvent` and dispatch it, triggering the listener.

Exercise 2: Non-Bubbling Event

Task: Create a custom event `"update"` that does not bubble, dispatch it on a child `div`, and verify it's not caught by a listener on the parent.

HTML:
```
<div id="parent">
  <div id="child"></div>
</div>
```

Solution:
```
const parent =
document.getElementById('parent');
const child =
document.getElementById('child');
parent.addEventListener('update', () => {
  console.log('Parent received update');
});
child.addEventListener('update', () => {
  console.log('Child received update');
});
const updateEvent = new
CustomEvent('update', { bubbles: false });
child.dispatchEvent(updateEvent);
// Output: "Child received update" only, no
parent message.
```

Explanation:
Because `bubbles: false`, the event does not bubble up to the parent.

Exercise 3: Cancelable Event

Task: Create a cancelable custom event `"action"` and call `event.preventDefault()` in the listener. Check the return value of `dispatchEvent()`.
Solution:
```
document.addEventListener('action', (e) =>
{
  e.preventDefault();
});
const actionEvent = new
CustomEvent('action', { cancelable: true
});
const result =
document.dispatchEvent(actionEvent);
console.log(result); // false, since event
was canceled
```
Explanation:
`dispatchEvent()` returns false if `preventDefault()` was called on a cancelable event.

Exercise 4: Stopping Propagation

Task: Add two listeners to the same element for a `"testEvent"`. In the first listener, call `event.stopImmediatePropagation()`. Confirm the second listener is not called.
Solution:
```
const div =
document.getElementById('someDiv');
div.addEventListener('testEvent', (e) => {
  console.log('First listener');
  e.stopImmediatePropagation();
});
```

```
div.addEventListener('testEvent', () => {
  console.log('Second listener');
});
const testEvent = new Event('testEvent', {
bubbles: true });
div.dispatchEvent(testEvent);
// Output: "First listener" only
```
Explanation:
`stopImmediatePropagation()` stops further listeners
on the same element.

Exercise 5: Passing Complex Data

Task: Dispatch a custom event `"data-ready"` from
window with detail `{ items: [1,2,3] }`. Listen and
log the items.
Solution:
```
window.addEventListener('data-ready', (e)
=> {
  console.log('Items:', e.detail.items); //
[1,2,3]
});
const dataEvent = new CustomEvent('data-
ready', {
  detail: { items: [1, 2, 3] }
});
window.dispatchEvent(dataEvent);
```
Explanation:
We used `window` as the event target and passed a complex
object in `detail`.

Exercise 6: Bubble a Custom Event Up the DOM

Task: Dispatch a custom event `"notify"` from a child element with `bubbles: true`. Listen for it on the parent element.

HTML:

```
<div id="parent">
  <div id="child"></div>
</div>
```

Solution:

```
const parent =
document.getElementById('parent');
const child =
document.getElementById('child');
parent.addEventListener('notify', (e) => {
  console.log('Parent caught notify');
});
const notifyEvent = new
CustomEvent('notify', { bubbles: true });
child.dispatchEvent(notifyEvent);
// Output: "Parent caught notify"
```

Explanation:

With `bubbles: true`, the event travels up to the parent listener.

Exercise 7: Custom Event on Document for Global Communication

Task: Dispatch a `"user-logged-in"` event from one part of the code and handle it in another, logging the username from `detail`.

Solution:

```
// Listener (could be in another
file/module)
document.addEventListener('user-logged-in',
(e) => {
```

```
  console.log('User logged in:',
e.detail.username);
});
// Dispatching the event
const loginEvent = new CustomEvent('user-
logged-in', {
  detail: { username: 'john_doe' }
});
document.dispatchEvent(loginEvent);
// Output: "User logged in: john_doe"
```
Explanation:
Using document, we can communicate globally across modules.

Exercise 8: Canceling an Event and Checking Result

Task: Create a "check" event that is cancelable. In a listener, conditionally call preventDefault(). Log dispatchEvent()'s return to see if it was canceled.
Solution:
```
document.addEventListener('check', (e) => {
  const condition = true; // Suppose
condition is true
  if (condition) e.preventDefault();
});
const checkEvent = new CustomEvent('check',
{ cancelable: true });
const wasNotCanceled =
document.dispatchEvent(checkEvent);
console.log(wasNotCanceled); // false if
preventDefault() was called
```

Explanation:
`preventDefault()` on a cancelable event makes `dispatchEvent()` return false.

Exercise 9: Different Event Targets

Task: Dispatch a `"refresh"` event from an element `#refreshBtn`, and catch it on `document`.
HTML:
```
<button id="refreshBtn">Refresh</button>
```
Solution:
```
const refreshBtn =
document.getElementById('refreshBtn');
document.addEventListener('refresh', () =>
{
  console.log('Refresh event caught on
document');
});
const refreshEvent = new Event('refresh', {
bubbles: true });
refreshBtn.dispatchEvent(refreshEvent);
// Output: "Refresh event caught on
document"
```
Explanation:
Bubbling allows the event from `refreshBtn` to reach `document`.

Exercise 10: Using stopPropagation() in a Custom Event Scenario

Task: Create a custom event `"child-action"` on a child `div`. Listen on both child and parent. In the child listener, call `stopPropagation()` to prevent the parent from handling it.

HTML:
```
<div id="parentDiv">
  <div id="childDiv"></div>
</div>
```
Solution:
```
const parentDiv =
document.getElementById('parentDiv');
const childDiv =
document.getElementById('childDiv');
parentDiv.addEventListener('child-action',
() => {
  console.log('Parent received child-
action');
});
childDiv.addEventListener('child-action',
(e) => {
  console.log('Child received child-
action');
  e.stopPropagation();
});
const childActionEvent = new
CustomEvent('child-action', { bubbles: true
});
childDiv.dispatchEvent(childActionEvent);
// Output: "Child received child-action"
only
```
Explanation:
stopPropagation() prevents the event from reaching the parent.

Conclusion

By understanding custom events and how to dispatch, listen, and pass data with them, you can build more modular and decoupled architectures. They enable components to communicate without direct references, promoting maintainability and scalability. Experiment with different configurations (`bubbles`, `cancelable`) and apply these concepts to create responsive, event-driven applications.

JavaScript: Window and Document Objects

The `window` and `document` objects are fundamental to working with the browser's environment in JavaScript. Together, they let you access browser features, control windows and tabs, manipulate the webpage (DOM), and interact with the user's screen.

Introduction to the Window Object

The **window object** represents the browser window or tab. It is the global object in a browser environment, meaning variables and functions not declared inside another scope become properties and methods of `window`. Many APIs, like `alert`, `console`, and `setTimeout`, are accessible via `window`.

Example:

```
// These two are equivalent:
window.alert('Hello');
```

```
alert('Hello');
// Global variable:
var x = 10;
console.log(window.x); // 10
```

Window Methods and Properties

Common Window Methods

- `alert(message)`: Displays an alert box.
- `confirm(message)`: Displays a modal dialog with OK/Cancel.
- `prompt(message, default)`: Displays a prompt dialog.
- `setTimeout(function, milliseconds)`: Calls a function after a delay.
- `setInterval(function, milliseconds)`: Calls a function repeatedly at intervals.
- `clearTimeout(timeoutID)`, `clearInterval(intervalID)`: Cancel timeouts/intervals.
- `open(url, target, features)`: Opens a new browser window or tab.
- `close()`: Closes the current window (if opened by script).
- `scrollTo(x, y)`: Scrolls the window to a given position.
- `requestAnimationFrame(callback)`: Schedules a repaint.

Common Window Properties

- `window.innerWidth` / `window.innerHeight`:
Viewport dimensions.
- `window.outerWidth` / `window.outerHeight`:
Browser window outer dimensions.
- `window.location`: Returns a `Location` object for the current URL.
- `window.history`: Access and navigate the browser history.
- `window.navigator`: Information about the browser and operating system.
- `window.screen`: Screen object with screen-related properties.

Example:
```
console.log('Window inner width:',
window.innerWidth);
console.log('User Agent:',
window.navigator.userAgent);
```

Screen Properties

The `window.screen` object provides information about the user's screen:
- `screen.width` and `screen.height`: The total screen width/height in pixels.
- `screen.availWidth` and `screen.availHeight`:
The available screen space.
- `screen.colorDepth`: The number of bits used to display colors.
- `screen.pixelDepth`: The pixel depth of the screen.

Example:
```
console.log('Screen width:', screen.width);
```

```
console.log('Screen height:',
screen.height);
console.log('Color depth:',
screen.colorDepth);
```

The Document Object

The **document object** represents the entire HTML document loaded in the browser. It's the root node of the DOM and provides methods and properties for selecting elements, modifying content, and interacting with the user.
Example:
```
console.log(document.title); // Get the
title of the page
document.title = "New Title"; // Set a new
title
```

Document Properties and Methods

Common Document Properties

- `document.title`: The text in the `<title>` element.
- `document.URL`: The URL of the current document.
- `document.domain`: The domain of the document.
- `document.body`: The `<body>` element.
- `document.head`: The `<head>` element.

Selection Methods

- `document.getElementById(id)`: Select an element by its ID.
- `document.getElementsByTagName(tag)`: Returns an HTMLCollection of elements by tag.
- `document.getElementsByClassName(class)`: Returns an HTMLCollection by class.
- `document.querySelector(selector)`: Returns the first element matching a CSS selector.
- `document.querySelectorAll(selector)`: Returns a NodeList of all matches.

Creating and Modifying Elements

- `document.createElement(tagName)`: Create a new element.
- `document.createTextNode(text)`: Create a new text node.
- `element.appendChild(node)`, `element.removeChild(node)`: Modify the DOM structure.
- `element.innerHTML`, `element.textContent`: Set or get HTML/text content.

Example:

```
const p = document.createElement('p');
p.textContent = 'Hello World!';
document.body.appendChild(p);
```

Multiple Choice Questions

Question 1

Which object represents the browser window in JavaScript?

- A) `document`
- B) `window`
- C) `screen`
- D) `history`

Answer: B) `window`

Explanation: The `window` object represents the browser window/tab.

Question 2

Which property would you use to get the entire width of the user's screen?
- A) `window.innerWidth`
- B) `screen.width`
- C) `screen.availWidth`
- D) `document.width`

Answer: B) `screen.width`

Explanation: `screen.width` gives the total screen width in pixels.

Question 3

Which method displays a message and waits for the user to press OK/Cancel?
- A) `alert()`
- B) `confirm()`
- C) `prompt()`
- D) `message()`

Answer: B) `confirm()`

Explanation: `confirm()` displays a modal with OK/Cancel buttons.

Question 4

Which property of the document returns the `<body>` element?
- A) `document.body`
- B) `document.main`
- C) `document.html`
- D) `document.container`

Answer: A) `document.body`

Explanation: `document.body` references the `<body>` element of the document.

Question 5

To get the current URL of the page, use:
- A) `document.URL`
- B) `window.URL`
- C) `location.href`
- D) `document.locationURL`

Answer: C) `location.href`

Explanation: `location.href` gives the current URL; `document.URL` also gives the page URL, but `location.href` is more commonly used.

Question 6

`document.querySelector('.className')` returns:
- A) The first element with that class
- B) A list of all elements with that class
- C) An HTMLCollection
- D) The last element with that class

Answer: A) The first element with that class

Explanation: `querySelector()` returns only the first match.

Question 7

Which method creates a new HTML element?
- A) `document.createNewElement()`
- B) `document.createElement(tagName)`
- C) `document.newElement(tagName)`
- D) `document.buildElement(tagName)`

Answer: B) `document.createElement(tagName)`
Explanation: This is the standard method to create an element node.

Question 8

To remove a child node, you use:
- A) `element.removeChild(childNode)`
- B) `element.deleteChild(childNode)`
- C) `document.remove(childNode)`
- D) `window.removeNode(childNode)`

Answer: A) `element.removeChild(childNode)`
Explanation: `removeChild()` is the method for removing a specific child node from its parent.

Question 9

`window.alert('Hello')` and `alert('Hello')` are:
- A) Different, `window.alert()` is safer
- B) Identical in effect
- C) Deprecated methods
- D) Only `alert('Hello')` works

Answer: B) Identical in effect
Explanation: `alert` is a global method and can be called with or without `window.` prefix.

Question 10

Which property returns the current domain of the document?
- A) `document.URL`
- B) `document.hostname`
- C) `document.domain`
- D) `location.domain`

Answer: C) `document.domain`

Explanation: `document.domain` returns the domain name of the server.

Question 11

To repeatedly call a function every 2 seconds, use:
- A) `setTimeout(func, 2000)`
- B) `setInterval(func, 2000)`
- C) `requestAnimationFrame(func)`
- D) `window.schedule(func, 2000)`

Answer: B) `setInterval(func, 2000)`

Explanation: `setInterval()` runs the function repeatedly at the specified interval.

Question 12

`document.getElementById('myId')` returns:
- A) A single element or null if not found
- B) A NodeList of all matched elements
- C) An HTMLCollection of matched elements
- D) A string with the ID's name

Answer: A) A single element or null if not found

Explanation: `getElementById()` always returns the single unique element with that ID.

Question 13

`document.getElementsByTagName('p')` returns:
- A) A NodeList
- B) An HTMLCollection
- C) An array
- D) A single element

Answer: B) An HTMLCollection

Explanation: `getElementsByTagName` returns an HTMLCollection.

Question 14

To stop a setInterval, you need the interval ID and call:
- A) `clearInterval(intervalID)`
- B) `stopInterval(intervalID)`
- C) `intervalID.clear()`
- D) `cancelInterval(intervalID)`

Answer: A) `clearInterval(intervalID)`

Explanation: `clearInterval()` is used to stop a repeating interval.

Question 15

`prompt('Enter name:')` returns:
- A) Boolean
- B) The input string or null if canceled
- C) Always a string
- D) Undefined

Answer: B) The input string or null if canceled

Explanation: `prompt()` returns what the user typed or null if the user canceled.

Question 16

Which of these accesses the browser history?
- A) `window.document`
- B) `window.history`
- C) `window.navigator`
- D) `window.screen`

Answer: B) `window.history`

Explanation: The `history` object allows navigation through the browser history.

Question 17

`document.head` returns:
- A) The `<head>` element
- B) The `<body>` element
- C) All meta tags
- D) Undefined

Answer: A) The `<head>` element

Explanation: `document.head` references the `<head>` node.

Question 18

To open a new browser window:
- A) `window.open(url, target, features)`
- B) `document.openWindow(url)`
- C) `navigator.open(url)`
- D) `screen.open(url)`

Answer: A) `window.open(url, target, features)`

Explanation: `window.open()` opens a new browsing context.

Question 19

`screen.availWidth` gives:
- A) The width of the screen excluding the taskbar
- B) The same as `screen.width`
- C) Always 0
- D) The width in CSS pixels only

Answer: A) The width of the screen excluding the taskbar

Explanation: `availWidth` excludes interface features like the taskbar.

Question 20

`document.querySelectorAll('.class')` returns:
- A) An HTMLCollection
- B) A NodeList
- C) An array
- D) A single element

Answer: B) A NodeList

Explanation: `querySelectorAll()` returns a NodeList of all matches.

10 Coding Exercises with Solutions

Exercise 1: Get and Change Document Title

Task: Log the current document title and then change it to "New Page Title".

Solution:
```
console.log(document.title);
document.title = "New Page Title";
```
Explanation:
`document.title` can read or write the page title.

Exercise 2: Selecting an Element by ID

Task: Assume there's an element `<div id="container"></div>` in the HTML. Select it and add text "Hello" inside it.
Solution:
```
const container =
document.getElementById('container');
container.textContent = 'Hello';
```
Explanation:
`getElementById` finds the element, then `textContent` sets its text.

Exercise 3: Query Selecting a Class

Task: Given multiple `<p class="text">` elements, select all of them and log their count.
Solution:
```
const paragraphs =
document.querySelectorAll('.text');
console.log(paragraphs.length);
```
Explanation:
`querySelectorAll('.text')` returns a NodeList of all `.text` elements.

Exercise 4: Creating and Appending an Element

Task: Create a new `<li>` element with text "New Item" and append it to an existing `<ul id="myList">`.
Solution:
```
const ul =
document.getElementById('myList');
const li = document.createElement('li');
li.textContent = 'New Item';
```

```
ul.appendChild(li);
```
Explanation:
createElement creates the li, appendChild inserts it into the ul.

Exercise 5: Using setTimeout

Task: After 2 seconds, display an alert saying "Time's up!".
Solution:
```
setTimeout(() => {
  alert("Time's up!");
}, 2000);
```
Explanation:
setTimeout delays execution of the callback by the specified milliseconds.

Exercise 6: Using confirm

Task: Ask the user a yes/no question: "Do you want to continue?" and log the user's response.
Solution:
```
const answer = confirm("Do you want to
continue?");
console.log(answer ? "User chose OK" :
"User chose Cancel");
```
Explanation:
confirm returns true if OK, false if Cancel.

Exercise 7: Scroll the Window

Task: Scroll the window to top-left corner (0,0) after a button click.
Solution:

```
// Assume a button with id="scrollBtn"
document.getElementById('scrollBtn').addEve
ntListener('click', () => {
  window.scrollTo(0, 0);
});
```
Explanation:
`window.scrollTo(0,0)` moves the viewport to the top-left corner.

Exercise 8: Get Screen Properties

Task: Log the screen width and height to the console.
Solution:
```
console.log('Screen Width:', screen.width);
console.log('Screen Height:',
screen.height);
```
Explanation:
Access `screen.width` and `screen.height` directly.

Exercise 9: Using prompt

Task: Prompt the user for their name and then display an alert greeting them by name.
Solution:
```
const name = prompt("What is your name?");
if (name !== null) {
  alert(`Hello, ${name}!`);
}
```
Explanation:
`prompt` returns the entered string or null if canceled.

Exercise 10: document.querySelector vs. document.querySelectorAll

Task: Select the first <h1> in the document using `querySelector` and all <p> tags using `querySelectorAll`. Log their counts.

Solution:

```
const firstH1 =
document.querySelector('h1');
console.log(firstH1 ? "H1 found" : "No H1
found");
const allPs =
document.querySelectorAll('p');
console.log(`Number of paragraphs:
${allPs.length}`);
```

Explanation:

`querySelector` returns a single element, `querySelectorAll` returns a NodeList.

Conclusion

Understanding `window` and `document` objects is essential for client-side development. They offer the functionality to interact with the browser environment and the web page's content. With these tools, you can create dynamic, interactive, and responsive user experiences.

JavaScript: Browser API Integration

Modern web browsers provide powerful APIs that allow developers to access and use device capabilities and system-level features. By integrating these APIs into your

JavaScript applications, you can create more interactive, accessible, and user-friendly experiences.

Geolocation API

The **Geolocation API** enables you to obtain the geographic location of a user's device. This can be used for maps, location-based services, and more.

Key Methods:

- `navigator.geolocation.getCurrentPosition(successCallback, errorCallback, options)`
- `navigator.geolocation.watchPosition(successCallback, errorCallback, options)`
- `navigator.geolocation.clearWatch(watchId)`

Example:

```
if ("geolocation" in navigator) {
  navigator.geolocation.getCurrentPosition(
    (position) => {
      console.log("Latitude:",
position.coords.latitude);
      console.log("Longitude:",
position.coords.longitude);
    },
    (error) => {
      console.error("Error:",
error.message);
    }
  );
} else {
  console.log("Geolocation not supported");
}
```

Common Options:

- `enableHighAccuracy`: Boolean for high-accuracy results.
- `timeout`: Max time in ms to wait.
- `maximumAge`: Accept a cached position up to a certain age in ms.

Web Speech API

The **Web Speech API** provides two interfaces:
- **SpeechSynthesis** (Text-to-Speech)
- **SpeechRecognition** (Speech-to-Text)

Text-to-Speech (SpeechSynthesis):

```
const utterance = new
SpeechSynthesisUtterance("Hello, how are
you?");
speechSynthesis.speak(utterance);
```

Speech-to-Text (SpeechRecognition) (in Chrome and some browsers):

```
const recognition = new
window.SpeechRecognition();
recognition.onresult = (event) => {
  const transcript =
event.results[0][0].transcript;
  console.log("Heard:", transcript);
};
recognition.start();
```

Note: Web Speech Recognition is not widely supported in all browsers.

Web Notifications API

The **Notifications API** allows you to display system-level notifications to the user.
Requesting Permission:

```
Notification.requestPermission().then(permi
ssion => {
  if (permission === "granted") {
    new Notification("Hello!", { body:
"Welcome back." });
  }
});
```

Creating a Notification:

```
if (Notification.permission === "granted")
{
  new Notification("Notification Title", {
    body: "This is a notification body",
    icon: "icon.png"
  });
}
```

Notification Events:

```
const n = new Notification("Title", { body:
"Content" });
n.onclick = () => {
  console.log("Notification clicked");
};
```

Web Workers

Web Workers allow you to run JavaScript in a separate background thread, preventing heavy computations from blocking the main UI thread.

Creating a Worker:

Create a separate JavaScript file, for example `worker.js`:

```javascript
// worker.js
self.onmessage = (e) => {
  const result = e.data.num * 2;
  self.postMessage(result);
};
```

Use it in the main script:

```javascript
const worker = new Worker('worker.js');
worker.onmessage = (e) => {
  console.log("Result from worker:",
e.data);
};
worker.postMessage({ num: 10 }); // Send
data to worker
```

Terminating a Worker:

• `worker.terminate()` stops the worker immediately.

SharedWorker and ServiceWorker exist but have different lifecycles and scopes.

Multiple Choice Questions

Question 1

Which API allows you to obtain the user's latitude and longitude?
- A) Web Workers
- B) Notifications API
- C) Geolocation API
- D) Web Speech API

Answer: C) Geolocation API
Explanation: The Geolocation API provides latitude and longitude data.

Question 2

`navigator.geolocation.getCurrentPosition(success, error, options)` is used for:
- A) Getting the user's location once
- B) Continuously watching user's position
- C) Translating speech to text
- D) Sending system notifications

Answer: A) Getting the user's location once
Explanation: `getCurrentPosition` retrieves the current location once.

Question 3

Which API is used for speech synthesis (Text-to-Speech)?
- A) SpeechSynthesis in Web Speech API
- B) SpeechRecognition in Web Speech API
- C) Geolocation API
- D) ServiceWorker API

Answer: A) SpeechSynthesis in Web Speech API
Explanation: The `SpeechSynthesis` interface handles text-to-speech.

Question 4

What is needed before showing a system notification?
- A) No permission needed
- B) User's IP address
- C) Notification permission granted by the user
- D) Geolocation coordinates

Answer: C) Notification permission granted by the user
Explanation: The user must grant notification permission first.

Question 5

Which method continuously watch the user's location changes?
- A) `geolocation.getCurrentPosition()`
- B) `geolocation.watchPosition()`
- C) `geolocation.trackPosition()`
- D) `geolocation.followPosition()`

Answer: B) `geolocation.watchPosition()`
Explanation: `watchPosition` provides continuous updates.

Question 6

How to stop a Web Worker?
- A) `worker.stop()`
- B) `worker.terminate()`
- C) `worker.close()`
- D) `worker.end()`

Answer: B) `worker.terminate()`
Explanation: `terminate()` stops the worker.

Question 7

If `SpeechRecognition` is not defined, it implies:
- A) The browser doesn't support speech recognition
- B) The code is wrong
- C) Permissions were not granted
- D) The user is offline

Answer: A) The browser doesn't support speech recognition

Explanation: Not all browsers implement `SpeechRecognition`.

Question 8

To create a notification:
- A) `new Notification("Title")`
- B) `Notification.create("Title")`
- C) `alert("Title")`
- D) `NotificationsAPI("Title")`

Answer: A) `new Notification("Title")`

Explanation: `new Notification` creates a notification instance.

Question 9

`Notification.permission` returns:
- A) 'granted', 'denied', or 'default'
- B) true or false
- C) 'allowed' or 'blocked'
- D) 'yes' or 'no'

Answer: A) 'granted', 'denied', or 'default'

Explanation: These are the possible notification permission states.

Question 10

Web Workers run on:
- A) The main thread
- B) A separate background thread
- C) The server
- D) The GPU

Answer: B) A separate background thread
Explanation: Web Workers run in parallel to the main thread.

Question 11

To handle messages sent from the main script inside a worker, use:
- A) `self.onmessage`
- B) `window.onmessage`
- C) `document.onmessage`
- D) `worker.onmessage`

Answer: A) `self.onmessage`
Explanation: Inside the worker, `self` references the worker's global scope.

Question 12

Which property of `position.coords` gives the altitude?
- A) `coords.latitude`
- B) `coords.longitude`
- C) `coords.altitude`
- D) `coords.height`

Answer: C) `coords.altitude`
Explanation: `coords.altitude` provides altitude if available.

Question 13

To speak the text "Hello world", you'd use:
- A) `speechSynthesis.speak(new SpeechSynthesisUtterance("Hello world"))`
- B) `speechRecognition.speak("Hello world")`

- C) `geolocation.speak("Hello world")`
- D) `worker.speak("Hello world")`

Answer: A) `speechSynthesis.speak(new SpeechSynthesisUtterance("Hello world"))`

Explanation: `speechSynthesis` and `SpeechSynthesisUtterance` handle speech output.

Question 14

What must you call before showing notifications?
- A) `Notification.requestPermission()`
- B) `Notification.allow()`
- C) `Notification.enable()`
- D) `Notification.setup()`

Answer: A) `Notification.requestPermission()`

Explanation: This method asks the user for permission.

Question 15

`watchPosition()` returns an ID that can be cleared by:
- A) `navigator.geolocation.clear(id)`
- B) `navigator.geolocation.clearWatch(id)`
- C) `navigator.geolocation.stopWatch(id)`
- D) `navigator.geolocation.removeWatch(id)`

Answer: B) `navigator.geolocation.clearWatch(id)`

Explanation: Use `clearWatch()` to stop watching position changes.

Question 16

Speech recognition results are usually accessed via:
- A) `event.results`
- B) `event.transcript`

- C) `event.speechText`
- D) `event.detail`

Answer: A) `event.results`

Explanation: `SpeechRecognition` returns an array of `SpeechRecognitionResult` in `event.results`.

Question 17

A worker communicates with the main thread using:
- A) Global variables
- B) `postMessage()` and `onmessage`
- C) Shared memory by default
- D) Cookies

Answer: B) `postMessage()` and `onmessage`

Explanation: They communicate via message passing.

Question 18

If `Notification.permission` is `'default'`, it means:
- A) User has not granted nor denied permission yet
- B) Permission is granted
- C) Permission is denied
- D) Notifications are blocked by default

Answer: A) User has not granted nor denied permission yet

Explanation: 'default' means no explicit choice made by user yet.

Question 19

To handle speech recognition errors, listen to:
- A) `recognition.onerror`
- B) `recognition.onfail`

- C) `recognition.error`
- D) `recognition.onError()`

Answer: A) `recognition.onerror`

Explanation: `onerror` event handler is used for speech recognition errors.

Question 20

Which API might require a secure context (HTTPS) for full functionality?
- A) Geolocation API
- B) Web Speech API
- C) Notifications API
- D) All of the above

Answer: D) All of the above

Explanation: Most sensitive browser APIs require HTTPS for security reasons.

10 Coding Exercises with Full Solutions

Exercise 1: Get User's Current Position

Task: Log the user's current latitude and longitude.
Solution:

```
if ('geolocation' in navigator) {

navigator.geolocation.getCurrentPosition((p
os) => {
    console.log("Lat:",
pos.coords.latitude, "Lon:",
pos.coords.longitude);
  }, (err) => {
    console.error("Error:", err.message);
```

```
  });
} else {
  console.log("Geolocation not
supported.");
}
```
Explanation:
We check if `geolocation` is available and then use
`getCurrentPosition`.

Exercise 2: Continuous Geolocation Tracking

Task: Watch the user's position and log changes until
cleared after 10 seconds.
Solution:
```
let watchId =
navigator.geolocation.watchPosition((pos)
=> {
  console.log("Updated Pos:",
pos.coords.latitude, pos.coords.longitude);
}, (err) => {
  console.error(err);
});
setTimeout(() => {

navigator.geolocation.clearWatch(watchId);
  console.log("Stopped watching
position.");
}, 10000);
```
Explanation:
`watchPosition` gives continuous updates. `clearWatch`
stops updates.

Exercise 3: Simple Text-to-Speech

Task: Speak the phrase "Hello world" using the Web Speech API.
Solution:
```
const utter = new
SpeechSynthesisUtterance("Hello world");
speechSynthesis.speak(utter);
```
Explanation:
Create an utterance and speak it.

Exercise 4: Speech Recognition (if supported)

Task: Start speech recognition, log recognized text, and stop after one result.
Solution:
```
if ('SpeechRecognition' in window) {
  const recognition = new
window.SpeechRecognition();
  recognition.onresult = (event) => {
    const transcript =
event.results[0][0].transcript;
    console.log("Recognized text:",
transcript);
    recognition.stop();
  };
  recognition.start();
} else {
  console.log("Speech recognition not
supported.");
}
```
Explanation:
We check support, start recognition, and handle results.

Exercise 5: Request Notification Permission

Task: Ask user for notification permission and log the result.
Solution:
```
Notification.requestPermission().then(permi
ssion => {
  console.log("Notification permission:",
permission);
});
```
Explanation:
We must request permission before creating notifications.

Exercise 6: Show a Notification (if granted)

Task: Show a notification with a title and body if permission is granted.
Solution:
```
if (Notification.permission === 'granted')
{
  new Notification("Hello!", { body: "You
have a new message." });
} else {
  console.log("No permission to show
notification.");
}
```
Explanation:
Check Notification.permission before showing a notification.

Exercise 7: Create and Communicate with a Web Worker

Task: Create a worker that doubles a number. Send the number 5 and log the result.

worker.js:

```
self.onmessage = (e) => {
  const num = e.data;
  self.postMessage(num * 2);
};
```

main.js:

```
const worker = new Worker('worker.js');
worker.onmessage = (e) => {
  console.log("Result from worker:",
e.data); // Should log 10
};
worker.postMessage(5);
```

Explanation:
We send data to the worker and receive processed data back.

Exercise 8: Stop a Web Worker

Task: After receiving one result from the worker, terminate it.

Solution:

```
const worker = new Worker('worker.js');
worker.onmessage = (e) => {
  console.log("Result:", e.data);
  worker.terminate();
  console.log("Worker terminated");
};
worker.postMessage(5);
```

Explanation:
We terminate the worker after getting the first message.

Exercise 9: High-Accuracy Geolocation

Task: Get position with `enableHighAccuracy: true`.
Solution:
```
navigator.geolocation.getCurrentPosition((p
os) => {
  console.log("High accuracy position:",
pos.coords);
}, null, { enableHighAccuracy: true });
```
Explanation:
We pass options to get more accurate location data if
available.

Exercise 10: Notification click event

Task: Create a notification and log a message when it's
clicked.
Solution:
```
if (Notification.permission === 'granted')
{
  const n = new Notification("Click me", {
body: "Click to do something" });
  n.onclick = () => {
    console.log("Notification clicked!");
  };
}
```
Explanation:
We add an `onclick` event listener to the notification.
By integrating Browser APIs like Geolocation, Web Speech,
Notifications, and Web Workers, you can build richer,
more interactive web applications. These APIs allow you to
tap into the device's hardware and capabilities, make your
application responsive and personalized, and improve user
experience. The provided examples, questions, and

exercises give you a strong foundation to begin using these powerful features in your projects.

Conclusion

Congratulations on completing **"JavaScript DOM Manipulation"**! You've taken a significant step toward mastering the art of creating dynamic and interactive web applications. From understanding the structure of the DOM to implementing complex event-driven behaviors, you now possess the tools to build scalable and efficient web solutions.

Your journey with the DOM doesn't end here—it's a gateway to exploring advanced topics like **React, Vue.js, and Angular**, which rely on DOM manipulation principles. Continue practicing, experimenting, and applying what you've learned to your projects. Remember, the key to growth lies in consistent exploration and hands-on coding. Thank you for embarking on this learning journey. Stay curious, and don't hesitate to revisit this book as a reference for future projects. The world of JavaScript awaits your innovation.

About the Author

Laurence Lars Svekis is a distinguished web developer, sought-after educator, and best-selling author, renowned for his profound contributions to JavaScript development and modern programming education. With over two decades of experience in web application development, Laurence has become a leading authority in the field, empowering a global audience with his clear, insightful, and practical approach to complex coding concepts.

As a **Google Developer Expert (GDE)**, Laurence is celebrated for his work with **Google Apps Script**, where he creates innovative solutions for automation, workflow optimization, and custom app development. His expertise extends beyond Google technologies, with a deep mastery of **JavaScript, functional programming, asynchronous programming, and front-end web development**. This unique combination of skills allows him to deliver comprehensive courses and resources that simplify even the most challenging programming concepts.

Laurence has educated over **one million students worldwide** through his **interactive courses, books, and live presentations**. His approach to teaching revolves around simplicity, clarity, and hands-on learning, making advanced topics like **closures, asynchronous programming, and functional programming** accessible to learners at all levels. His content is enriched with **real-world examples, coding exercises, and projects** designed to solidify key concepts.

In addition to his online courses, Laurence is a prolific author. His books offer readers an immersive learning experience with practical coding exercises, multiple-choice quizzes, and detailed explanations. These resources serve as an essential guide for developers seeking to master **JavaScript fundamentals and advanced topics** and write clean, maintainable, and scalable code.

Laurence's impact on the developer community is immense. As an active participant in the **Google Apps Script and JavaScript developer communities**, he regularly engages with learners, shares insights, and fosters collaboration among developers. His ability to bridge technical complexity with clear, step-by-step guidance has made him a trusted voice in the world of JavaScript education.

Through his books, courses, and live presentations, Laurence inspires developers to unlock their potential, refine their skills, and achieve career success in the fast-evolving world of software development. His influence extends far beyond traditional teaching, offering a fresh perspective on how **education, development, and innovation** intersect.

To learn more about his work and discover a treasure trove of free resources, visit **BaseScripts.com**, where Laurence's passion for teaching, coding, and community building continues to shape the next generation of developers.

www.ingramcontent.com/pod-product-compliance
Lightning Source LLC
LaVergne TN
LVHW051233050326
832903LV00028B/2389